Christianity in Crisis
Christ's Plan for Recovery

Christianity in Crisis
Christ's Plan For Recovery

Moody Adams

Christianity in Crisis
Christ's Plan for Recovery

Christianity in Crisis
Christ's Plan for Recovery

"If ye love me, keep my commandments"
(John 14:15).

Christianity in Crisis
Christ's Plan for Recovery

Christianity in Crisis
Christ's Plan For Recovery

First Edition
© 2010 by Moody Adams Evangelistic Association, Inc.

ISBN: 978-0-9725915-5-3

Scripture quotations are from
The Holy Bible, King James Version (KJV) unless contained in quotations

COPYRIGHT & FAIR USE POLICY
All rights are reserved by the publisher, but readers are encouraged to quote material from this book for reviews or teaching purposes, on condition the quote is not longer than 500 words and is not the primary content of a work being sold; that the contents are not altered; and that credit is properly given to the source. For additional usage guidelines, email the Publisher at:
moodyadams@moodynews.com

The Moody Adams Evangelistic Association, Inc.
11715 Bricksome Avenue, Suite B-3
Baton Rouge, Louisiana 70816
Telephone: 225-291-7333
Fax: 225-291-0103
E-mail: moodyadams@moodynews.com
Web: www.moodynews.com

Christianity in Crisis
Christ's Plan for Recovery

Contents

Foreword 9
Chapter 1 Facing our Crisis 11
Chapter 2 The Forgotten Commission 15
Chapter 3 Let Your Light Shine Before Men 19
Chapter 4 Rejoice Always 23
Chapter 5 Repent 27
Chapter 6 Follow Me 29
Chapter 7 Get Right With Others Before Giving Your Money ...31
Chapter 8 Be Perfect 33
Chapter 9 Do Not Commit Adultery 37
Chapter 10 Swear Not 41
Chapter 11 Do Not Resist Evil 43
Chapter 12 Turn the Other Cheek 47
Chapter 13 Respond to a Law Suit With Generosity 49
Chapter 14 Go the Second Mile 51
Chapter 15 Love Your Enemies 53
Chapter 16 Bless Them that Curse You 55
Chapter 17 Do Good to Them That Hate You 57
Chapter 18 Pray for Them That Despitefully use You 59
Chapter 19 Do Not Give Money To Impress People 61
Chapter 20 Secure Your Treasures in Heaven 65
Chapter 21 Seek God's Kingdom First 69
Chapter 22 Judge Not 71
Chapter 23 Clear Your Own Eyes Before You Seek To Help Others 75

Christianity in Crisis
Christ's Plan for Recovery

Christianity in Crisis
Christ's Plan for Recovery

Chapter 24 Do Not Offer the Gospel to Reprobates 77
Chapter 25 Treat Others as You Want to be Treated 81
Chapter 26 Ask, Seek, and Knock in Prayer 83
Chapter 27 Travel the Narrow Way 85
Chapter 28 Beware of False Prophets 89
Chapter 29 Pray for More Laborers 91
Chapter 30 Be Wise and Harmless 95
Chapter 31 Take the Yoke With Christ 97
Chapter 32 Honor Your Parents 99
Chapter 33 Settle Disputes 101
Chapter 34 Despise Not The Little Ones 105
Chapter 35 Never Stop Forgiving 107
Chapter 36 Do Not Divorce 109
Chapter 37 Always Tell the Truth 111
Chapter 38 Guard Against False Teachings 113
Chapter 39 Pray With Faith 117
Chapter 40 Render to Caesar And God What is There's 119
Chapter 41 Be a Servant to Others 121
Chapter 42 Love the Lord 125
Chapter 43 Love Your Neighbor 129
Chapter 44 Be Ready for Christ's Return 131
Chapter 45 Watch for Christ's Return 133
Chapter 46 Observe the Lord's Supper 135
Chapter 47 Baptize My Disciples 139
Chapter 48 Proclaim the Gospel 141
Chapter 49 Make Disciples Among all Nations 143
Chapter 50 Practice Self-Denial 145
Chapter 51 Keep Yourself From Covetousness 149
Chapter 52 Feed the Poor 151
Chapter 53 Exercise Humility 153
Chapter 54 Make The Church A House of Prayer 155
Chapter 55 Receive the New Birth 159
Chapter 56 Feed My Sheep 161

Christianity in Crisis
Christ's Plan for Recovery

Christianity in Crisis
Christ's Plan for Recovery

Foreword

by Robert Funderburk

In the fifties, when I was ten, I went to a war movie at a neighborhood theatre(one screen.) A soldier passed his buddy sitting on the hood of a jeep, asking, "Why's the motor running?" His buddy replied, "Only way I can keep my tail warm." I was shocked, stunned that language like "tail" would be used in a movie. We were not a church-going family at the time.

America was "innocent" during those years. Bad people still did bad things, but society as a whole recognized them as "bad," including the people who did them. Some acts were considered shameful and social control kept them to a minimum; some were considered unworthy to discuss in polite company. Women and old folks were shown respect, children were treasured, marriage was considered inviolate, wives took care of the home and men provided for and protected the family. Divorce was rare. The safest place on Earth was a mother's womb. We were one nation under God.

Is this idealized? Somewhat. Did everyone live like this? Of course not. Were some parents abusive? Yes. But this was the norm before the "enlightenment" that began in the mid-sixties.

Molech. At times, God's chosen people, Israel, burned their children before this heathen god. Today in America, we burn our children inside the womb with a saline solution, or cut them to pieces inside the womb or with just the head protruding, drive a metal tube into the base of the skull and siphon out the baby's brains. Offerings to Molech. A reporter asked Mother Theresa if she thought western civilization was destroying

Christianity in Crisis
Christ's Plan for Recovery

itself. She replied, "When a mother will murder her own child, what's left to destroy?"

Homosexuality is portrayed by the elite media as an acceptable if not preferred lifestyle. The Bible clearly states that homosexuals, "shall not inherit the Kingdom of God." A pastor with one of the largest congregations in this nation was asked on national television how he handled this subject (sin) in his sermons. He replied, "I don't go there." Is this the bedrock problem in America? Are we a nation of politically correct pulpits? Are we afflicted by a gaggle of pastors and evangelists who,"…don't go there."

I make no judgment of anyone in any circumstance, but pray that the Holy Spirit will, "Lead you in all truth."

My prayer for America comes from the book of Isaiah 9:2 "The people who walk in darkness will see a great light; those who live in a dark land, the light will shine on them."

Christianity in Crisis
Christ's Plan for Recovery

Chapter 1

Facing Our Crisis

Hurricane Katrina launched an outbreak of looting in New Orleans. My granddaughter's husband, Stewart Hawkins, who served on a SWAT team, was ordered to the city to try and control the violence. He said it was frightening to listen to gun shots going off all night. The SWAT teams were in New Orleans to stop the looting in this predominantly Christian city. GlobalBeatz.net ran an article titled, "Christian 'looters' destroy sex shops in New Orleans."

By contrast, in the greater tsunami catastrophe in Japan there was virtually no looting. "Foreign observers are noting with curiosity and wonder why the Japanese people in disaster-plagued areas are not looting for desperately-needed supplies like bottled water," writes Thomas Lifson in The Thinker magazine. Something is terribly wrong when pagan morality is producing a higher morality than Christianity. The problem is not the men in Washington. The problem is the people who put them there. America's people have chosen many leaders who have forsaken God, because they have forsaken God.

There are three clear signs that a nation has forsaken God and is in crisis. The Lord established these three institutions; the family, the church and the government. When a country forsakes God, all three deteriorate. This was clear in Israel after the death of Joshua. It is obvious today in the Western World.

The family declines

The home of Micah demonstrates the breakdown of the family in Ephraim. Micah steals his own mother's money, deceives his mother and then the two of them mold an idol god.

Christianity in Crisis
Christ's Plan for Recovery

"The birth rate **IN THE U.S**. ... has gone from about 150,000 illegitimate babies in 1950 to 1,150,000 in 1990: **AN ASTRONOMICAL** rise, even considering population growth. ...The U.S. Census Bureau reported that almost 25% of the nation's unmarried women become mothers, and that just over the past decade there has been a 60% increase in births out of wedlock (De Parle, 1993). ... recent estimates put the national illegitimacy rate at 30%...roughly 50% of marriages end in divorce...approximately one million American children per year have been involved in divorce" (http://www.catholiceducation.org/articles/marriage/mf0002.html).

Thirty seven percent of abortions are performed on Protestant Christians. Thirty one percent is performed on Catholics. Sixty eight percent of all abortions are performed on professing Christians, whose faith teaches this is wrong.

The religion declines

Micah corrupted the religion of Jehovah. He built his own little temple. It was so far to go to Shiloh to worship. He molded his own gods. He employed him his own preacher " (Judges 17:9-13). All this was to get the Lord "to do him good" (Judges 17:13). This clearly meant he would have health and wealth.

So many Christians are leaving the church, that this generation is being labeled as the "ex-Christian generation."

Ninety five percent of 20 to 29 year old evangelicals attended church regularly during their elementary and middle school years but only 11 percent of them were still regularly attending church when in college, according to a stunning survey by America's Research Group).

And it is not in the U.S. alone. Researchers say religion is set for extinction in nine countries. Religion will all but die out altogether in nine countries: Australia, Austria, Canada, the Czech Republic, Finland, Ireland, the Netherlands, New Zealand and Switzerland.

Christianity in Crisis
Christ's Plan for Recovery

German Chancellor Angela Merkel stirred her audience and won a 10 minute standing ovation, when she spoke at her conservative party's conference in Karlsruhe on Monday. "Germany doesn't suffer from too much Islam, but too little Christianity," she said.

While the numbers of Western Christians attending church is declining, large numbers of those still going to church are abandoning basic Christian beliefs. USAToday recently reported on a recent survey that found 52 percent of American Christians believe that eternal life is not exclusively for those who accept Jesus Christ as their Savior.

"The Secular Student Alliance, which promotes atheism and humanism with chapters at more than 200 colleges, is sending in reinforcements for teen free-thinkers -- a push to launch 50 new high school clubs," reports Cathy Lynn Grossman in USA TODAY. These atheist clubs are glorying in their 250 clubs.

St. Timothy's United Methodist Church in Cedar Falls, Iowa, presented, "Jesus, Mary and...Josephine?' This was a lesbian Nativity at their church.

ABC affiliate KTRK, in Houston, announced, "Women in the Houston area are pole dancing once a month...for Jesus. Yes, the dance moves, once reserved for strip clubs, are being embraced by devout, church-going women called "pole fitness for Jesus."

A survey by Christianity Today revealed 37 percent of pastors said pornography is a "current struggle" of theirs.

Morality declines

Morals were ruined. Everyman decided for himself what was right and wrong. They wanted no rules controlling what they could do. "In those days there was no king in Israel, but every man did that which was right in his own eyes" (Judges 17:6). Micah's godlessness spread into the tribe of Dan (Micah 18).

An article titled, "Lie, Cheat and Steal: High School Ethics Surveyed [Excerpts]" says, "In the past year, 30 percent of U.S. high school

Christianity in Crisis
Christ's Plan for Recovery

students have stolen from a store and 64 percent have cheated on a test. The Josephson Institute, a Los Angeles-based ethics institute, surveyed 29,760 students. Their anonymity was assured. Michael Josephson, the institute's founder and president, said he was most dismayed by the findings about theft. The survey found that 35 percent of boys and 26 percent of girls--30 percent overall--acknowledged stealing from a store within the past year." The survey also revealed 64 percent of students cheated on a test in the past year.

TV news in Massachusetts informs us that U.S. students report they are being awakened and distracted from their studies by their roommates engaged in sex in their dorm room!

A first-of-its-kind study released by the Centers for Disease Control and Prevention shows 1 in 4 teenage girls in the United States has a sexually transmitted disease.

Even those practicing the wickedness of Sodomy consider themselves Christians. Homosexual web sites advertisements read:

Gay Christian Dating

Find Gay Christian Men

Christian Hook-Ups for Single Gays

These problems are all the result of one failing: the church is only carrying out half of the Great Commission. Christ has a recovery plan for us, but it is not easy.

Chapter 2

The Forgotten Commission

The Command

"Teaching them to observe all things whatsoever I have commanded you" (Matthew 28:20).

The Meaning

The problems of our morals, families churches and nation are all the result of one thing, the church is only carrying out half the great commission. Jesus not only said to "Go ye into all the world, and preach the gospel to every creature." (Mark 16:15). He also commissioned the church to "Teaching them to observe all things whatsoever I have commanded you" (Matthew 28:20).

There is one thing unifying all Christians—one thing they all have in common. Protestant and Catholic, Calvinist and Armenian, Charismatic and non-charismatic, denominational and Independent, contemporary and traditional have all ignored this command.

Masses of Western Christians have no interest in obeying Christ commands; most do not even know His commands. They cherish His offer of forgiveness, mercy and eternal life, so they are offered these things with no mention of the need to obey Christ.

Western Christianity resembles the pagans on Mount Olympus. They worshipped vigorously, but their gods were immoral and made no moral demands of their worshippers.

The godly A.W. Tozer aptly said, "Have you noticed how much praying for revival has been going on of late -- and how little revival has resulted? I believe the problem is that we have been trying to substitute praying for obeying, and it simply will not work. To pray for revival

Christianity in Crisis
Christ's Plan for Recovery

while ignoring the plain precept laid down in Scripture is to waste a lot of words and get nothing for our trouble. Prayer will become effective when we stop using it as a substitute for obedience." (http://www.pietyhilldesign.com/gcq/quotepages/obedience.html).

Henry T. Blackaby, Southern Baptist's spokesman on "Experiencing God" writes, "If Southern Baptists want to see a 'Great Commission Resurgence,' they need to focus on the relationship between disciples and the living Lord Jesus, not just launch a new emphasis on evangelism. "I have felt for a long time that Southern Baptists have focused on evangelism and missed discipleship" Blackaby told the Baptist Press on May 11, 2009. "The most important part of the Great Commission is to teach them to practice everything I have commanded you.' That's discipleship and that's the heart of the Great Commission."

Obedience is not a condition of salvation, but a result of salvation. Obeying my wife's commands was not a condition of marriage, but a result of marrying her and loving her.

Michael Craven said, "On the one hand we have conservative Christians who want a king without a kingdom (privatized salvation without any public affect) and on the other, liberal Christians who want a kingdom without a king (utopian schemes apart from Christ). Both are products of misunderstanding at best and apostasy at worst." (S. Michael Craven is the President of the Center for Christ & Culture. Michael is the author of Uncompromised Faith: Overcoming Our Culturalized Christianity, Navpress).

Jesus asked a disturbing quest of those who praise Him in pious tones, but do not obey Him: "And why call ye me, Lord, Lord, and do not the things which I say? (Luke 6:46).

Obedience is the way we show Christ our love for Him: "He that hath my commandments, and keepeth them, he it is that loveth me" (John 14:21).

Christianity in Crisis
Christ's Plan for Recovery

It is sad that some misguided souls enjoy going to church services, and singing, in soft religious tones of love for Jesus and immediately leaving the services with little consideration for obeying Christ.

The Christian's delight is to obey his Lord, just as the bride delights in obeying the bridegroom. Her greatest thrill is doing things that please her husband. If ye love me, keep my commandments" (John 14:15). "For the love of Christ constraineth us; because we thus judge, that if one died for all, then were all dead: And that he died for all, that they which live should not henceforth live unto themselves, but unto him which died for them, and rose again' (II Corinthians 5:14, 15).

God foresaw a day when false prophets would declare there was no need to obey Christ's commandments and wrote: "And hereby we do know that we know him, if we keep his commandments. He that saith, I know him, and keepeth not his commandments, is a liar, and the truth is not in him. But whoso keepeth his word, in him verily is the love of God perfected: hereby know we that we are in him" (I John 2:3-5).

Some oppose even the thought of obedience, declaring grace has set them free from such responsibility. But Christians are not free to do what they want, but free from the bondage of sin too do what Christ wants. "For there are certain men crept in unawares , who were before of old ordained to this condemnation, ungodly men, turning the grace of our God into lasciviousness (a license to sin).

This book contains the 55 Commandments of Christ that are the key to transforming lives, families, and our nation. Study them, learn them and obey them. This is the only way back to God.

The Example
A nobleman in Cana of Galilee asked Jesus to come to his house and heal his sick son. "The nobleman saith unto him, Sir, come down ere my child die. Jesus saith unto him, Go thy way ; thy son liveth" (John 4:50). The noble obeyed Jesus command, without seeing a thing happen. When he returned home he found his son had been healed. **Such is the reward of obedience.**

Christianity in Crisis
Christ's Plan for Recovery

Chapter 3

Let Your Light Shine Before Men

The Command

"Let your light so shine before men, that they may see your good works, and glorify your Father which is in heaven" (Matthew 5 16).

The command is to "let your light shine" to glorify our Lord Jesus by your godly life.

The Meaning

In a dark world of evil, Christians are commanded to be a light that shows their unselfish works and glorifies their heavenly Father: "Let your light so shine before men, that they may see your good works, and glorify your Father which is in heaven" (Matthew 5:16). Look at men stumbling around in this dark evil world

Jesus made Christians a light in this dark world, just as a man lights a candle in a dark house. Christians are made lights to shine in a world lost in darkness and show their good works.

Matthew Henry cried , "Let them see your good works, that they may see the power of God's grace in you, and may thank him for it, and give him the glory of it, who has given such power unto men. With motives of piety. Let them see your good works, that they may be convinced of the truth and excellency of the Christian religion, may be provoked by a holy emulation to imitate your good works, and so may glorify God". (http://www.apostolic-churches.net/bible/mhc/matthew/5.html).

Christianity in Crisis
Christ's Plan for Recovery

A small light shows up more brilliantly the darker the night is. Likewise, the darker the times, the more corrupt the world, the more brilliantly a Christian life stands out.

Sometimes we feel like escaping as David felt, when he cried, "And I said , Oh that I had wings like a dove! for then would I fly away , and be at rest" (Psalm 55:6). Sometimes, we would like to be monks, get away from the crowds, live alone away from the stresses of life. The problem is, Christ commands us to this opposite.

This world likes to hear about Christians doing charitable work, but cares little about hearing about the source—Jesus Christ. Jesus is the power of Christian benevolence and acts of charity. To perform them without declaring Christ as the source, may feel good, but it is not giving glory to Christ, but rather to self.

Allan Davis wisely wrote, "The true Christian life is not about "theatrical goodness." Jesus criticized the Pharisees for performance-based religion. They routinely fasted, gave tithes of all they had flagellated themselves, wore signs of their piety on their clothes and heads (verses written on parchment were bound in rolls called "phylacteries" and worn on their foreheads) and did organized works of charity. They did it to be seen and admired or respected by others" (Matthew 6:1; 23:5).

Examples

As newsman Clarence W. Hall followed American troops through Okinawa in 1945, he and his jeep driver came upon a small town that stood out as a beautiful example of a Christian community. He saw many villages that were devastated and discouraged. There was this one where the people were happy, smiling and giving dignified bows. They took pride in showing off their "terraced fields, spotless homes, storehouses and granaries and the prized sugar mill."

"Hall said that he saw no jails and no drunkenness, and that divorce was unknown in this village. He was told that an American missionary had come there some 30 years earlier. While he was in the village, he had led two elderly townspeople to Christ and left them with a Japanese Bible. These new believers studied the Scriptures and started leading their fellow villagers to Jesus. Hall's jeep driver said he was amazed at the difference between this village and the others around it. He remarked, "So this is what comes out of only a Bible and a couple of old guys who wanted to live like Jesus" (http://www.free-sermons.org/sermons/Let-Your-9110).

Christianity in Crisis
Christ's Plan for Recovery

Chapter 4

Rejoice Always

The Command

Christ commanded, "Rejoice, and be exceeding glad" (Matthew 5:11-12).

Meaning

Paul repeated this command to the Philippian Christians, "Finally, my brethren, rejoice in the Lord" (Philippians 3:1). Again, he writes to the Thessalonians, "Rejoice evermore" (I Thessalonians 4:1). It is the responsibility of all true Christians to continually "rejoice," to demonstrate to other Christians the meaning of true Christian joy. The key to obeying this command is to focus on "the Lord." "Rejoice in the Lord." If you rejoice in:
- a sporting victory, the next game could be a devastating defeat;
- financial gain, that could all be lost;
- feeling good, a tiny bacteria could destroy your health;
- a fine family, death can break it up in a moment.

If, however, your joy is in the eternal Lord, nothing can take it away—never. When our rejoicing is over the benefit of our God's power, faithfulness, love, mercy, we can "rejoice always."

Bill Roberts says he knew a preacher who began every prayer by saying, "Thank you Lord for all the bad things that have not happened to me today."

Christians can rejoice that they are becoming holier during times of suffering. "For they verily for a few days chastened us after their own pleasure ; but he for our profit, that we might be partakers of his

Christianity in Crisis
Christ's Plan for Recovery

holiness. Now no chastening for the present seemeth to be joyous, but grievous: nevertheless afterward it yieldeth the peaceable fruit of righteousness unto them which are exercised thereby" (Hebrews 12:10, 11).

Puritan pastor Abraham Wright said, "I am mended by my sickness, enriched by my poverty, and strengthened by my weakness. What fools we are, then, to frown upon our afflictions! They are not indeed for our pleasure, they are for our profit." Christians rejoice that, though their pathway is painful, it leads to heaven: "For I reckon that the sufferings of this present time are not worthy to be compared with the glory which shall be revealed in us" (Romans 8:18).

Example

Dr. George W. Truett told of a Christian girl who married an ungodly unbeliever: "This dear girl, a wonderful Christian, was wooed and won by a handsome young fellow, but since he was a scorner of the things of God, she went into that atmosphere. His parents and his grandparents were also strong unbelievers. …The most insidious attacks were made on her faith, from everyone, but she remained calm, steadfast and true to Jesus. She had to make her way to the house of God alone.

"One day, as she moved about her duties in the kitchen, her clothing caught fire. …she died a few hours later. …She bore her sufferings with all the outstanding devotion of some mighty martyr for God. Not a word of reproach or bitterness escaped her lips. She went on quoting God's powerful and precious promises to the last.

"When it was evident to her that she was dying, she stretched out her charred, blackened, once beautiful hands and arms, and tried to put them around her husband's neck, and said: "Poor Charlie, the thing that tries me, and the only thing, about going away, is that I have not lived long enough to teach you and your dear parents and dear grandparents that Jesus is real.

"Then she passed away. The funeral was conducted, and her body was laid to rest. The family returned home; the day died down to nightfall; the bereaved ones sat by the open fire. Presently the young husband stirred and said to his father and grandfather, "Mary had what the rest of us do not have; I am going to seek her Saviour." The old grandfather stirred, came over to his son and grandson, and laid his hand on the head of each and said, "My sons, you are right. Mary did have what the rest of us do not have, and I am going to seek her Saviour, too." In three days, those men found Christ, as did several of their loved ones. This little woman who was called to pass through the vale of deepest darkness and suffering honored her God through it all. Her testimony was irresistible" (quoted by Homer Duncan in The purpose of Suffering).

Christianity in Crisis
Christ's Plan for Recovery

Christianity in Crisis
Christ's Plan for Recovery

Chapter 5

Repent

The Command

"Repent: for the kingdom of heaven is at hand" (Matthew 4:17).

The Meaning

Simply put "Repentance" means to be so sorry for your sins that you turn away from them.

Joel explained repentance well: "Therefore also now, saith the LORD, turn ye even to me with all your heart, and with fasting, and with weeping, and with mourning: And rend your heart, and not your garments, and turn unto the LORD your God: for he is gracious and merciful, slow to anger, and of great kindness, and repenteth him of the evil." (Joel 2:12. 13).

Isaiah exhorts us to, "Let the wicked forsake his way, and the unrighteous man his thoughts: and let him return unto the LORD, and he will have mercy upon him; and to our God, for he will abundantly pardon" (Isaiah 55:7).

Ezekiel assures us of the reward of repentance, "But if the wicked turn from his wickedness, and do that which is lawful and right, he shall live thereby" (Ezekiel 33:10).

Christians are not perfect. None of us can undo all the wrongs and hurts we have done to others, intentionally or otherwise. However, we must make right the things we can.

Christianity in Crisis
Christ's Plan for Recovery

The Example

This story is from Africa and was told by Festo Kivengere, an Anglican Archbishop said his uncle, the rich, tribal chief, had a man come to give him eight cows. He said he had stolen four from the chief and they had increased.

The chief asked, "Who arrested you?" "Jesus arrested me, sir," the man replied.

"There was no laughter, only a shocked silence. My uncle could see this man was at peace with himself and rejoicing. 'You can put me in prison or beat me up,' the man said, 'but I am liberated. Jesus came my way, and I am a free human being.' 'Well, if God has done that for you, who am I to put you in prison? You go home.'

" A few days later, having heard the news, I went to see my uncle. I said to him, 'Uncle, I hear you got eight free cows!' 'Yes, it's true,' he said. "You must be happy.' 'Forget it! Since that man came, I can't sleep. If I want the peace he has, I would have to return a hundred cows!'" Kivengere says that later his uncle came to Christ. (full story at http://www.christianity.co.nz/repent2.htm).

Chapter 6

Follow Me

The Command

"Then said Jesus unto his disciples, If any man will come after me, let him deny himself, and take up his cross, and follow me." (Matthew 16:24)

The Meaning

Jesus explained that to be His disciple there are three things a man must do: First, "Let him deny himself." This is a hard lesson. You cannot be a Christian and do what you want to do. Second, "take up his cross." You must take up a cross. The crucifix on a necklace will not suffice. Third, "Follow me" Jesus said. If you put your feet in the footprints of Jesus and follow them they will not lead to worldly fame and riches. They will lead you to Calvary, the place of crucifixion. Calvary is where you die—die to yourself, your goals, your pleasures, as signified by your 'burial' in baptism.

C.S. Lewis declared, "The terrible thing, the almost impossible thing, is to hand over your whole self--all your wishes and precautions--to Christ."

A.W. Tozer said: "Among the plastic saints of our times, Jesus has to do all the dying, and all we want to hear is another sermon about his dying."

The Example

"The frail Polycarp, white-haired Bishop of Smyrna, followed Jesus quite literally. He was drug into a Roman arena in about 155 AD. The crowd was crying for the death of Christians.

Christianity in Crisis
Christ's Plan for Recovery

"When the magistrate pressed him, and said, 'Swear, and I will release you; revile Christ,' Polycarp said, 'Eighty-six years have I been serving him, and he has done me no wrong; how then can I blaspheme my king who saved me?' "[22]

His final prayer, before they burned him to death was: "...wherefore I praise you also for everything; I bless you, I glorify you, through the eternal high priest, Jesus Christ, your beloved Son, through whom, with him, in the Holy Spirit, be glory unto you, both now and for the ages to come, Amen."

Christianity in Crisis
Christ's Plan for Recovery

Chapter 7

Get Right With Others Before Giving Your Money

The Command

"Leave there thy gift before the altar, and go thy way; first be reconciled to thy brother, and then come and offer thy gift. " (Mathew 5:24).

The Meaning

Jesus said to be reconciled to our Christian brothers before we give our offerings. Our relationship with God requires a proper relationship with our fellow Christians.

"Therefore if thou bring thy gift to the altar, and there rememberest that thy brother hath ought against thee; Leave there thy gift before the altar, and go thy way ; first be reconciled to thy brother, and then come and offer thy gift. Agree with thine adversary quickly, whiles thou art in the way with him; lest at any time the adversary deliver thee to the judge, and the judge deliver thee to the officer, and thou be cast into prison" (Matthew 5:23- 25).

"Though we are unfitted for communion with God, by a continual quarrel with a brother, yet that can be no excuse for the omission or neglect of our duty: "Leave there thy gift before the altar, lest otherwise, when thou has gone away, thou be tempted not to come again. (http://biblecommenter.com/matthew/5-25.htm).

This echoes the Old Testament instructions to the Jewish worshipper. When a worshipper brought his offering to the rail which separated him from the priest, he was to stop and see if he remembered if some brother had a charge against him. If so, he was not to give the

Christianity in Crisis
Christ's Plan for Recovery

offering, until he first went to the offender first and was reconciled with him.

The Church of England has a directive to this effect in her Communion service. Members are instructed reconciled to their fellow Christians before taking the Lord's Supper.

Jesus gave an example of what can occur when we fail to obey His order to be reconciled: "Agree with thine adversary quickly, whiles thou art in the way with him; lest at any time the adversary deliver thee to the judge, and the judge deliver thee to the officer, and thou be cast into prison" (Matthew 5:25).

Example

Dale Carnegie told about a disagreement he had over letting his dog run loose. The magistrate had warned him not to let his dog off the leach, in the park But one afternoon he decided to take a chance and took Rex's leash off. The dog took off running over a hill and headed straight for the magistrate. Carnegie said: "Officer, you've caught me red-handed. I'm guilty. I have no alibis, no excuses. You warned me last week that if I brought the dog out here again without a muzzle you would fine me."

"Well, now," the policeman replied. "I know it's a temptation to let a little dog like that have a run out here when nobody is around."

"Sure it's a temptation," Carnegie replied, "but it is against the law."

"Well, a little dog like that isn't going to harm anybody," the policeman remonstrated.

"No, but he may kill squirrels," Carnegie said. "Well now, I think you are taking this a bit too seriously," the magistrate said. "I'll tell you what you do. You just let him run over the hill there where I can't see him and we'll forget all about it."

The policeman got the respect he and the law demanded. Carnegie got out of a fine. He pulled this off by quickly admitting he was wrong and his adversary was right. Had he argued, he could have ended up paying a fine. Worse still, it could have escalated into an angry confrontation that would have ended with Carnegie being hauled off to jail.

Chapter 8

Be Perfect

The Command

"Be ye therefore perfect, even as your Father which is in heaven is perfect" (Matthew 5:48).

The Meaning

Perfection must always be the ambition, the goal, of the obedient Christian. He works toward it in this world and achieves it in the next.

Christ commanded us to desire, aim at and press towards perfection. In this world, there are no perfect people, but it is the desire of true Christians to be perfect and to pursue perfection. In this particular passage, it commands that we be perfect in our treatment of enemies, which is the current subject. "It is God's perfection to forgive injuries and to entertain strangers, and to do good to the evil and unthankful, and it will be ours to be like him. We that owe so much, that owe our all, to the divine bounty, ought to copy it out as well as we can" says Matthew Henry

There are many passages expanding our drive toward perfection. I Peter 1:15, 16, tells us to conform to the example of our heavenly father in holiness: "But as he which hath called you is holy, so be ye holy in all manner of conversation; Because it is written, Be ye holy; for I am holy."

God promises to sanctify us completely and preserve our whole spirit, soul and body blameless before him at his coming. (I Thessalonians 5:23, 24). We are told to pursue this perfecting of holiness, "Having therefore these promises, dearly beloved, let us cleanse

Christianity in Crisis
Christ's Plan for Recovery

ourselves from all filthiness of the flesh and spirit, perfecting holiness in the fear of God" (II Corinthians 7:1).

Our Lord also promises to put His laws in our hearts, and write them in our minds (Hebrews 10:16). Jesus is able to save to the uttermost those who come to God through Him (Hebrews 7:25) and "cleanse us from all unrighteousness" (1 John 1:9). God is able to "purify our hearts by faith" (Acts 15:9), "perfect, strengthen, settle and establish us" (1 Peter 5:10).

"Therefore, having these promises, beloved, let us cleanse ourselves from all filthiness of flesh and of spirit, perfecting holiness in the fear of God." (2 Corinthians 7:1)

A question has arisen regarding holiness. Some think if they quit drinking, gambling and chasing women they are perfect. These are only a few baby steps towards perfection. Christ is perfection. Anyone who says he has reached sinless perfection is saying he is as good as Jesus Christ. This, of course, is obviously untrue. I John 1:10 says, "If we say that we have not sinned, we make Him a liar and His world is not in us."

Example

The Apostle Paul cried, "I am crucified with Christ: Nevertheless I live; yet not I, but Christ liveth in me" (Galatians 2:20). This was a man who sought perfection. Wesley described such a man as follows: "He is 'holy as God who called' him 'is holy,' both in heart and 'in all manner of conversation.' He 'loveth the Lord his God with all his heart,' and serveth him 'with all his strength.' He 'loveth his neighbour,' every man, 'as himself;' yea, 'as Christ loveth us;' them, in particular, that 'despitefully use him and persecute him, because they know not the Son, neither the Father.' Indeed his soul is all love, filled with 'bowels of mercies, kindness, meekness, gentleness, longsuffering.' And his life agreeth thereto, full of 'the work of faith, the patience of hope, the labour of love.' "And whatsoever' he 'doeth either in word or deed,' he 'doeth it all in the name,' in the love and power, 'of the Lord Jesus.'" (http://gbgm-umc.org/umw/wesley/perfection.stm).

Christianity in Crisis
Christ's Plan for Recovery

Chapter 9

Do Not Commit Adultery

The Command
Matthew 5:27 commands, "...thou shalt not commit adultery."

The Meaning
Jesus said, "Ye have heard that it was said by them of old time, Thou shalt not commit adultery: But I say unto you, That whosoever looketh on a woman to lust after her hath committed adultery with her already in his heart. And if thy right eye offend thee, pluck it out, and cast it from thee: for it is profitable for thee that one of thy members should perish, and not that thy whole body should be cast into hell. And if thy right hand offend thee, cut it off, and cast it from thee: for it is profitable for thee that one of thy members should perish , and not that thy whole body should be cast into hell" (Matthew 5:27-30).

Matthew Henry's Commentary defines adultery as follows: "Do not commit adultery; for our chastity should be as dear to us as our lives, and we should be as much afraid of that which defiles the body as of that which destroys it. This commandment forbids all acts of uncleanness, with all those fleshly lusts which produce those acts and war against the soul, and all those practices which cherish and excite those fleshly lusts, as looking, in order to lust, which, Christ tells us, is forbidden in this commandment" (Matthew 5:28).

Jesus taught that those who look with lust "have" committed adultery in their hearts. Millions of American Christians proclaim like the rich young ruler, "all these have I kept from my youth up" (Matthew

Christianity in Crisis
Christ's Plan for Recovery

19:20). They never dream that they have broken this rule by lust. This command teaches us how desperately we all need the Lord Jesus Christ's atoning blood to save us.

Bishop J. C. Ryle asks, "What man or woman upon earth can ever stand before such a God as this, and plead 'not guilty'? Who is there that has ever grown to years of discretion, and not broken the commandments thousands of times? 'There is none righteous, no not one.' (Romans 3:10.) Without a mighty Mediator we should everyone be condemned in the judgment day." (http://www.youversion.com/notes/40722/matthew).

Today, adultery has become so popular, that web sites are promoting and profiting from it. They will help you arrange to meet someone desiring for extramarital sex. Here, are three such web sites:

"Commit Adultery" We'll Help You Get The Arrangement You Want, Easily and Discreetly.

"Married and Lonely" Local wives looking for a discrete affair. Free to search profiles!

"Adultery" Married People Looking For Affairs. View Profiles 100% Free. Join Now!

Another ad is circulating on the Internet advertising sex partners entitled "Just Hookup — For sex partners in your area."

One sites promises to refund your money if you do not have sex with one of their participants.

Example

Few people have ever been tempted to commit adultery like Joseph. This remarkable young man was in charge of the Egyptian king's house. One day his master's wife asked him to go to bed with her. She repeatedly tried to seduce him. Joseph refused. One day when they were in the house along, she grabbed hold of his robe and tried to drag him into her bed saying, "come to bed with me," But Joseph escaped and ran outside, and left his robe in her hand (Genesis 39:6-12). Joseph ended up in prison after she accused him of trying to rape her. Joseph could have given in to her seduction, enjoyed having sex and escaped prison.

Why did this young man refuse to commit adultery? Fear of getting caught? No. Fear of getting a disease? Fear the woman would get pregnant? No. When a desire is this strong these things are inadequate forces for stopping the act. What was Joseph's motivation? He said to the woman, "How then can I do this great wickedness, and sin against God? (Genesis 39:9). He recognized that the great crime of adultery was "a sin against God."

Christianity in Crisis
Christ's Plan for Recovery

Chapter 10

Swear Not

The Command

"But I say unto you, Swear not at all; neither by heaven; for it is God's throne" (Matthew 5:34).

The Meaning

This is a commandment against lying and swearing to it—to false swearing.

Matthew Henry says, clearly, the command means, "That we must not swear at all, but when we are duly called to it."

John Gill's Exposition of the Bible explains: "Some of our extreme brethren, like the Society of Friends, will never swear at all, even in a court room. We should not think for a moment that this is what Jesus commanded."

"Opposition to oath-taking caused many problems for these groups throughout their history. Quakers were frequently imprisoned because of their refusal to swear loyalty oaths. The United States has permitted affirmations since it was founded; it is explicitly mentioned in the Constitution. Only two US Presidents, Franklin Pierce and Herbert Hoover, have chosen to affirm rather than swear at their inaugurations." (Wikipedia Encyclopedia).

There are many Bible verses that not only allowing swearing, but even commanding us to swear: "Thou shalt fear the LORD thy God, and serve him, and shalt swear by his name" (Deuteronomy 6:13). Again in Deuteronomy 10:20, "Thou shalt fear the LORD thy God; him shalt thou

Christianity in Crisis
Christ's Plan for Recovery

serve, and to him shalt thou cleave, and swear by his name." Then Jeremiah 4:2 says, "And thou shalt swear, The LORD liveth, in truth, in judgment, and in righteousness; and the nations shall bless themselves in him, and in him shall they glory" (Jeremiah 4:2).

The Bible even says God swears, "I have sworn by myself, the word is gone out of my mouth in righteousness..." (Isaiah 45:23).

Some claim they are not lying if they have not sworn to something. This is what this command forbids.

Example

"Sir Tomas More was beheaded after refusing to swear an oath he thought dishonest. He was led from his cell in the Tower of London to Tower Hill where a crowd awaited his execution. More asks the crowd to pray for him in this world, and said he would pray for them in the next. He proclaimed he was "the King's good servant, but God's first." Then More kissed his executioner then knelt on the block, and was killed with one stroke of the axe. Afterwards, his head was boiled and put on a pole by London Bridge" (Famous Trials, by Douglas O. Linder (2011), University of Missouri-Kansas City School of Law).

Chapter 11

Do Not Resist Evil

The Command
Jesus commanded, in the sermon on the mount, "But I say unto you, That ye resist not evil" (Matthew 5:39)

The Meaning
One acid test of our Christianity is how we treat those who mistreat us. This refers to the evil others bring against you, not to that evil temptations that arise within you.

The Old Testament ordered an "eye for an eye" to limit punishment, lest a man would take two eyes for the one he had lost, or to kill a man who had cut off his arm. Jesus went beyond this limit on retribution for a wrong. He said do not resist the evil men do to you: "But I say unto you, That ye resist not evil: but whosoever shall smite thee on thy right cheek, turn to him the other also'" (Matthew 5:39).

Nothing shows us how Christ wants us to respond to evil better than the way He responded to those who abused Him and killed Him. When they mocked Him and cursed Him, Christ was as silent as a lamb before His shearers. When they beat Him with the whip and bloodied Him with their blows, Christ did not fight back. When they nailed Him to the cruel cross, Christ prayed that God would forgive them.

The book of Romans also explains what it means not to resist evil: "Recompense to no man evil for evil. Provide things honest in the sight of all men. If it be possible, as much as lieth in you, live peaceably with all men. Dearly beloved, avenge not yourselves, but rather give place unto wrath: for it is written, Vengeance is mine; I will repay, saith the

Christianity in Crisis
Christ's Plan for Recovery

Lord. Therefore if thine enemy hunger, feed him; if he thirst, give him drink : for in so doing thou shalt heap coals of fire on his head. Be not overcome of evil, but overcome evil with good" (Romans 12:17-21). Judgment is God's business. We must depend on Him and not try to play God by executing judgment ourselves.

By returning good for evil you "heap coals of fire" on the head of the one who did the evil. This is the legal, godly way to respond to evil. Return good. This is effective. By your kindness, you torture the evil doer by showing him what a dreadful person he is. It makes his conscience burn. He has to rethink doing evil because it is not producing the desired effect. You effectively overcome evil with good.

The Lord wants justice, but He wants the evil doers punished. God has given us governments to perform an imperfect form of justice now. He has set up a day of judgment to execute perfect justice in the future. We must depend on these and not execute judgment ourselves. This is God's business.

Jesus's command in Matthew 5 details how we are to return good for evil. In cases of:

1. Physical assault
2. Lawsuits
3. Compulsory service

"Who does not know that quarrelings, strifes, selfishness, and unkindness, causes half the miseries by which mankind is visited? Who can fail to see that nothing would so much tend to increase happiness as the spread of Christian love, such as is here recommended by our Lord?...true religion has the directly contrary effect: it tends to promote peace, and charity, and kindness, and goodwill among men," said J. C. Ryle.

Examples

Jay E. Adams relates: "A woman I was counseling whose husband

Christianity in Crisis
Christ's Plan for Recovery

was going away on weekends when he should have been with her decided that since he went away these weekends in camping that she would do something good for him instead of being furious and whining and complaining as she had been. So she started doing good. She'd pack weekend lunches. She'd put little surprises in his back pack. She would do all kinds of good things to make his weekend more pleasant. And it just changed everything in that home."

Attacking evil with 'good' is a more powerful weapon, than returning evil for evil could ever be!

Christianity in Crisis
Christ's Plan for Recovery

Christianity in Crisis
Christ's Plan for Recovery

Chapter 12

Turn the Other Cheek

The Command

"Jesus said, "But whosoever shall smite thee on thy right cheek, turn to him the other also" (Matthew 5:39).

The Meaning

It is easy to ignore this verse of scripture. However, it is a clear command of our Lord, not to be ignored if we love Jesus..

There are two extreme interpretations regarding the passage. One is by strict pacifists who would not fight anyone—even Hitler. If this view were correct and all followed it, Hitler would have conquered the world and continued his slaughter of "inferior races." The Allies stopped the Maxis from their murderous rampage by killing them. Pacifist make the mistake of not rightly dividing the Word of God (II Timothy 2:15). They do not divide God's rules for governments, from His rules for individuals. Governments have the right to take lives in order to prevent the slaughter of their own people. Scripture says "For rulers are not a terror to good works, but to the evil...he is the minister of God, a revenger to execute wrath upon him that doeth evil" (Romans 13:4). Evil is to be punished, but by the government, not by individuals.

On the other extreme, there are those who find no restriction on hitting back. They say the person in Christ's teaching is probably right handed and to strike the right side of another's face would be a mere slap meant to intimidate, not to hurt. The problem with this is, the point of the verse is not to resist evil, whether a mere slap or a hard blow, it is

Christianity in Crisis
Christ's Plan for Recovery

evil and must not be resisted. In addition, the passage says later you are to love your enemy.

If you want to hurt a man who hits you, then hit him back. But, if you want to hurt him far worse, return kindness for his blow. Then you "heap coals of fire on his head: "Therefore if thine enemy hunger, feed him; if he thirst, give him drink: for in so doing thou shalt heap coals of fire on his head" (Romans 12:20). You show an enemy, who has wronged you, that you are a far stronger person that he is. He knows he could not resist striking back. The strength of his blow only reveals the weakness of his character. What started as a show of strength becomes a declaration of his weakness.

The Examples

"Now, you might be wondering, does it work? Steven B. Curington answers. "A famous, eccentric Methodist preacher named Billy Bray tells of his remarkable conversion in his biography. He was an ex-miner and when he got saved and gave up his evil ways, his fellow minors were disgusted. One of them annoyed with him struck him in the face and stated, Take that for turning to Methody! After being struck, Billy compassionately looked at him and said, "May God forgive you man, as I do." Later the aggressive miner came to Christ. It was Billy's attitude that brought the man to Christ."

I was deeply impressed by the story of a young, Christian soldier who read his Bible and prayed every night by his bunk. One night a bully threw a boot and hit the Christian boy in the head. The next morning the bully awoke to find his boots beside his bunk, freshly polished. Shortly afterwards, the bully received Christ.

Chapter 13

Respond to a Law Suit With Generosity

The Command:

"And if any man will sue thee at the law, and take away thy coat, let him have thy cloak also" (Matthew 5:40).

The Meaning

Jesus' first example of evil was being struck on the cheek which was an attack on a person. The second regards an attack on property; someone suing you to take away your coat. The book of Luke records, "Him that taketh away thy cloke forbid not to take thy coat also" (Luke 6:29).

The "coat" was the most valuable possession of a poor Jew. It protected him from the sun's heat on warm days and the cold on winter's days. Scripture commanded, "If thou at all take thy neighbour's raiment to pledge, thou shalt deliver it unto him by that the sun goeth down: For that is his covering only, it is his raiment for his skin: wherein shall he sleep? and it shall come to pass, when he crieth unto me, that I will hear; for I am gracious" (Exodus 22:26-27).

So even though a man had a right to keep his coat, it was better if a contentious, cantankerous man goes to court and takes away his coat, that he give him your cloke also. It would be better to be stripped naked than to be involved in a contentious courtroom brawl.

"The merciful are happy. We must not only bear our own afflictions patiently, but we must do all we can to help those who are in misery. We must have compassion on the souls of others, and help them; pity those who are in sin, and seek to snatch them as brands out of the burning,"

Christianity in Crisis
Christ's Plan for Recovery

wrote Matthew Henry. Jesus is teaching us how to witness to a wicked world. We can impress them by such unusual acts of kindness to those who don't deserve it.

Paul wrote, "Now therefore there is utterly a fault among you, because ye go to law one with another. Why do ye not rather take wrong ? why do ye not rather suffer yourselves to be defrauded ?" (I Corinthians 6:7).

Examples

William Barclay gave this example of the command: "Churches are tragically full of people (who demand their rights), officials whose territory has been invaded, office-bearers who have not been accorded their proper place, courts which do business with a manual of practice and procedure on the table all the time, lest anyone's rights should be invaded. People like that have not even begun to see what Christianity is. The Christian thinks not of his rights, but of his duties; not of his privileges, but of his responsibilities" (http://www.pastortom.org/sm15.htm).

Christianity in Crisis
Christ's Plan for Recovery

Chapter 14

Go the Second Mile

The Command

Jesus said, "And whosoever shall compel thee to go a mile, go with him twain" (Matthew 5:41).

The Meaning

The third command against resisting evil regards your time — the first two was against your person, the second against your property and now an imposition upon your time.

Roman soldiers would often require people to carry their pack or shield. This placed a wearisome, time consuming burden on them. However, the soldiers had the authority to command whatever they wanted. When Jesus stumbled beneath the weight of the cross, Simon of Cyrene was "compelled" or "forced" to carry Jesus' cross by a Roman soldier?

Jesus said the way to handle this was to do more than you were asked — to carry the load a mile more than required. This would make a deep impression on the Roman soldier.

Suppose a cop stopped and ordered you to walk a line to prove you were sober. Afterwards, you might go over to his car and clean the windshield for him.

The command means stop thinking about yourself; your rights, your convenience, and think about showing the love of Christ to another.

Christianity in Crisis
Christ's Plan for Recovery

Example

    J.R. Rosado told this story about an old man. This gentleman was annoyed by the trash in front of his house: Tireless, he pick up the trash and tried to get the license plate number of the litterers. His doctor told him he had to get more exercise, so he started walking around the block. Sometimes he would pick up trash as he walked.

    The doctor was pleased with his improvement on his next appointment. He never explained what happen, but he was obviously a happier man.

    The big change took place following a sermon on, "You have heard that it was said, 'Eye for eye, and tooth for tooth.' But I tell you, Do not resist an evil person. If someone strikes you on the right cheek, turn to him the other also. And if someone wants to sue you and take your tunic, let him have your cloak as well. If someone forces you to go one mile, go with him two miles" (Matthew 5:38-41).

    That sermon resulted in the old man making a decision to go the second mile. Then he went down to the highway department and discussed his predicament. They had him fill out some paper work and a big change had started.

    The next time he visited his doctor, he was told, "Well, I was driving by your street and your house the other day, and I know why your health is better. With a tear in the doctor's eye, the doctor said, "and I think I'll stop throwing my Coca-Cola cans out the window." For you see the highway department had decided to put up a tribute sign. The sign read this: "the next two miles have been adopted by a 100 year old man...he wanted to remain anonymous but asked us to put up these eight words: please read Matthew five, verses thirty-eight through forty-two" (http://www.bibleguide.org/daily-living.html).

Chapter 15

Love Your Enemies

Perhaps this is the most difficult command Jesus ever gave. Nothing tests the realness of a person's faith like this passage. The verse contains four commands. The first is to love your enemies.

The Command
"But I say unto you, Love your enemies, bless them that curse you, do good to them that hate you, and pray for them which despitefully use you, and persecute you" (Matthew 5:44)

The Meaning
To love your enemies means far more than not mistreating them, refraining from retaliating against them, or not hurting them in any way. It means to have affection for them; to be concerned with their well being, to help them in any way; to assisting them in prospering. When a person receives Christ one of the notable changes is in his attitude toward his enemies. The unregenerate person hates his enemies and works to hurt them. The converted person is commanded to love his enemies, and by the power of the Holy Spirit, he can do this.

Here, is an acid test of true Christianity; "Do you really love your enemies? Are you obeying this command of Christ? Alistair Begg, senior pastor of Parkside Church in Chagrin Falls, Ohio, writes, "Ask yourself this question, whether in all honesty, we can say that the picture of whatever is evangelical Christianity in the public arena is a picture of people who apparently are taking seriously the phrase 'loved ones, never

Christianity in Crisis
Christ's Plan for Recovery

avenge yourselves.'" He mentioned that a local mediator in the Cleveland law courts told him that the worst cases she has dealt with involved Christian pastors. It is not easy, he admitted, to heed Paul's plea (as revealed in Romans 12). In fact, Begg believes not taking vengeance and being at peace with everyone 'is one of the hardest things in the whole of Christian living because it is completely antithetical to the way in which things work.'"

Seneca said: 'Live for thy neighbour if thou wouldst live for God'.

Christian scholars cut back flips trying to get out of obeying this plain command: "love your enemies."

The Example

When Abraham Lincoln was running for President, a Mr. Stanton said, "You don't want a tall, lanky, ignorant man like this as president of the United States." Stanton went about the country saying and writing vile things about Lincoln. When Lincoln was having to choose a Secretary of War, he mentioned Stanton's name to his advisors. They though the idea foolish and reminded Lincoln of the awful things the man had said about him. Lincoln replied, "Oh yes, I know about it; I read about it; I've heard him myself. But after looking over the country, I find that he is the best man for the job." When Lincoln was assassinated, Stanton made a terrific statement about the character of Lincoln and proclaimed: "Now he belongs to the ages" (http://www.sermoncentral.com/illustrations/sermon-illustration-mark-brunner-story.html).

Chapter 16

Bless Them that Curse You

The second command in the verse is to return blessing for cursing.

The Command
"But I say unto you, Love your enemies, bless them that curse you…" (Matthew 5:44).

The Meaning
When wicked men curse you, instead of returning evil for evil, say nice words about those who curse you. Return kind words for their evil cursing. This does not mean praising them, which would be shameful. It means to ask for a blessing upon those whose mouths are full of cursing and bitterness.

"Jesus teaches in Luke 6:27 that we are to bless those who curse us. Paul explains in Roman 12:14-21 that by blessing our enemies, we actually heap burning coals on their head.

John Wesley wrote, "Bless them that curse you - Speak all the good you can to and of them, who speak all evil to and of you. Repay love in thought, word, and deed, to those who hate you" (Luke 6:27, 35).

The Examples
I had a friend who was witnessing in New Orleans' French Quarters when a man spit in his face. My big, strong friend wiped it off and went on telling the man about Jesus as if nothing had happened.

Shimei cursed and belittled David: "Then Abishai son of Zeruiah said to the king, "Why should this dead dog curse my lord the king? Let me go over and cut off his head." But the king said, "What do you and I

Christianity in Crisis
Christ's Plan for Recovery

have in common, you sons of Zeruiah? If he is cursing because the LORD said to him, 'Curse David,' who can ask, 'Why do you do this?' " David then said to Abishai and all his officials, 'My son, who is of my own flesh, is trying to take my life. How much more, then, this Benjamite! Leave him alone; let him curse, for the LORD has told him to. It may be that the LORD will see my distress and repay me with good for the cursing I am receiving today'" (2 Samuel 16: 9-12).

    Shimei falsely accused David, saying God was judging him for sinning against the house of Saul, attributing David's circumstances and the loss of his kingdom to God's judgment for alleged past sins against the house of Saul. Abishai, David's bodyguard and nephew, wanted to retaliate and attack Shimei (Samuel 16:9). However, David restrained himself, responded humbly, and took Shimei's curse as from the Lord (2 Samuel 16:10-12).

Chapter 17

Do Good to Them That Hate You

The third command in this verse is to do good to those who hate you.

The Command

"But I say unto you, Love your enemies, bless them that curse you, do good to them that hate you..." (Matther 5:44).

The Meaning

True Christians are remarkably different from other people, even those in other religions. They show this in the way they treat other people. They don't treat others as they deserve, but with compassion, with forgiveness. This means that being a disciple of Jesus is not some nice, easy religion that makes no demands on your life. It is demanding. Jesus expects His followers to love their enemies.

Pick out your worst enemy; the person who has dealt you the most painful wrong. Now face the command of Jesus Christ and trust the Christ living in you to enable you to forgive. Then think of something you could do to prove to your enemy and yourself that you have forgiven.

This is not an unreasonable command. Think of all the things God has forgiven you of, so many, many sins. Remember He has even forgiven you of being His enemy.

The world does not think like our Lord. The Lord Jesus forbids anything resembling a revengeful spirit, an unforgiving heart, a

Christianity in Crisis
Christ's Plan for Recovery

quickness in taking offense, a quarrelsome and contentious attitude. These are all contrary to the mind of Christ.

The Example

I had a pastor friend who suffered a serious wrong at the hands of a man he had befriended. This friend, his music director, resigned the church, moved to a neighboring church and took their entire choir with him. It left the church devastated. It left the pastor worse than devastated. His whole life was consumed by this wrong he had suffered. When he discussed his grief with me, I advised him to forgive the man who had hurt him, to send him a nice present, write him a "wish you well" card and to get on with his life. He took the advice. That is what it means to obey Christ's command to do good to those who hate you.

Chapter 18

Pray for them That Despitefully use You

The fourth and final command in this one verse is to pray for those who are spitefully using you.

The Command

"But I say unto you, Love your enemies, bless them that curse you, do good to them that hate you, and pray for them which despitefully use you, and persecute you" (Matthew 5:44).

The Meaning

As long as we live, we will come across people who make life difficult for us. People will just use us for their own pleasure and benefit. There will be people who persecute us. Naturally, we pray for God to stop them from hurting us, and pray for strength to endure. We are commanded to "pray for them which despitefully use you, and persecute you." This means we are not to just pray about these people, but for them. We are to put up with a lot, rather than hurt another person, or cause offence. We are to be unselfish. We should not think, "how should I treat this person?" We should think, "How would Christ treat this person?" Take the person who has mistreated you the most. Have you forgiven this person? Are you nice to this person? Do you love this person?

The Example

As Jesus hung upon the cross, dying, He prayed for His killers and even made an excuse for them, "Father, forgive them, for they know not

Christianity in Crisis
Christ's Plan for Recovery

what they do." In His death, Jesus left us an example of how we must treat those who despitefully use us and persecute us. He prayed for them. Think of the suffering that Jesus must have been going through in the hours before his crucifixion and the painful death He was enduring, yet he still managed to pray for them: "Then said Jesus, Father, forgive them; for they know not what they do" (Luke 23:33, 34). Jesus chose to pray for His cruel killers to be pardoned from an eternal hell.

Christianity in Crisis
Christ's Plan for Recovery

Chapter 19

Do Not Give Money To Impress People

The Command

"Take heed that ye do not your alms before men" (Matthew 6:1).

The Meaning

Jesus stressed the importance of performing religious acts to impress God and not men. These include giving, praying and fasting. In Matthew 6, He said, Take heed that ye do not your alms before men, to be seen of them: otherwise ye have no reward of your Father which is in heaven. Therefore, when thou doest thine alms, do not sound a trumpet before thee, as the hypocrites do in the synagogues and in the streets, that they may have glory of men. Verily I say unto you, They have their reward. But when thou doest alms, let not thy left hand know what thy right hand doeth: That thine alms may be in secret: and thy Father which seeth in secret himself shall reward thee openly. And when thou prayest, thou shalt not be as the hypocrites are: for they love to pray standing in the synagogues and in the corners of the streets, that they may be seen of men. Verily I say unto you, They have their reward. But thou, when thou prayest, enter into thy closet, and when thou hast shut thy door, pray to thy Father which is in secret; and thy Father which seeth in secret shall reward thee openly...moreover when ye fast, be not, as the hypocrites, of a sad countenance: for they disfigure their faces, that they may appear unto men to fast. Verily I say unto you, They have their reward. But thou, when thou fastest, anoint thine head, and wash thy face; That thou appear not unto men to fast, but unto thy Father which is in secret: and

Christianity in Crisis
Christ's Plan for Recovery

thy Father, which seeth in secret, shall reward thee openly" (Matthew 6:1-18).

Hypocrisy is to pretend to be better than you are. Religious exercises must be to please God, not to please men. God commands us not to be as the hypocrites whose acts are to be seen of men. Modern hypocrites love to make a show of their spirituality, wearing clothes that denote their devotion to God, parading about the streets carrying crosses, and making long public prayers. A Christ forbids all of this.

Fredrick Crawford explains, "The 'theatrical' Christian uses the same important elements found within a theater environment. Elements included are the actors, script, audience, and building. The actors pretend to be people they are not, while attempting to convince the audience they are that person. A superb actor is convincing! The script allows the actors to maintain control of the events they are acting out. The audience comes to see a performance and wants to be entertained. The actors seek approval from their audience showing that the acting is convincing. This confirmation motivates the actors to keep on acting. The building in which performances take place keeps the outside out and the performance in. The outside of the building is typically uglier than the setting and atmosphere inside. The building is made up of props to make the stage look attractive and 'real'" (Theatrical Christians by Fredrick Crawford).

When it comes to being a Christian hypocrite, the actors are those professing to be Christians. They claim to be church members but are not doing anything unusual. They mostly sit in the pews on Sunday and wear crosses around their necks to go along with the flow of church. These people are merely acting out a script of carefully orchestrated words, decisions, and actions. Their words must be manageable to keep their lives comfortable, enjoyable, and orderly. The script definitely must be achievable, because the only play worth acting is a successful one.

"You hypocrites, rightly did Isaiah prophesy of you:" 'These people honor me with their lips, but their hearts are far from me. They worship

Christianity in Crisis
Christ's Plan for Recovery

me in vain; their teachings are but rules taught by men.'" (Matthew 15: 8-9).

The Example

"If there were an award for hypocrisy, Rev. Jesse Jackson would be a strong contender. During the dark days of Bill Clinton's Monica Lewinsky sex scandal, Jackson bravely dove into the media storm and paid a visit to the President to offer moral counseling. Jackson brought along staffer Karin Stanford, who was visibly pregnant.

"It turned out later that Jackson was the father of that child. To try to cover up his "little error," the good reverend used organizational money to arrange for his playmate to live in a home worth $345,000 and to receive $10,000 per month. Because Jesse Jackson is a darling of the liberal media, the magnitude of his hypocrisy was quickly lost by the press when it declared the whole affair resolved." (Jesse Jackson - by Todd Strandberg, http://www.pvpanther.com/news/2004/11/03/InTheSpirit/Christian.Hypocrisy-790619...).

Christianity in Crisis
Christ's Plan for Recovery

Chapter 20

Secure Your Treasures in Heaven

The command

"Lay not up for yourselves treasures upon earth, where moth and rust doth corrupt, and where thieves break through and steal :But lay up for yourselves treasures in heaven, where neither moth nor rust doth corrupt , and where thieves do not break through nor steal :For where your treasure is, there will your heart be also" (Matthew 6:19-21).

The Meaning

Christ said we should lay up our treasure in heaven. Use your money to glorify Jesus and help the needy in Jesus' name. This protects your money from moths, rust and thieves. This increases your treasures in heaven.

What is the Christian's heavenly treasure? It is: "To an inheritance incorruptible, and undefiled, and that fadeth not away, reserved in heaven for you," (1 Pet. 1:4).

Matthew Henry declares, "Worldly-mindedness is as common and as fatal a symptom of hypocrisy as any other, for by no sin can Satan have a surer and faster hold of the soul, under the cloak of a visible and passable profession of religion, than by this; and therefore Christ, having warned us against coveting the praise of men, proceeds next to warn us against coveting the wealth of the world."

Our hearts are attracted to treasure, just as a compass is unfailingly attracted to the north. Treasure on earth can corrupt our hearts. The Bible

Christianity in Crisis
Christ's Plan for Recovery

clearly tells us that wherever our wealth is, there our heart will be also: For where your treasure is, there will your heart be also" (Matthew 6:21).

Dr. James Merrit relates the story of a church in Atlanta that started selling chicken to help pay the bills. It was listed in the Yellow Pages as " Church of God Grill." The chicken sales made a lot of money and they finally closed the church, but kept the Grill and the name, "Church of God Grill." The heart follows the treasure, as the compass needle follows the north.

If we do not obey this commandment and put our treasure in heaven, money can becomes a master and no man can serve two masters: "No servant can serve two masters: for either he will hate the one, and love the other; or else he will hold to the one, and despise the other. Ye cannot serve God and mammon" (Luke 16:13)

"You can put your treasure in God, or you can put your treasure in chicken, but you can't do both. Once the chicken is eaten the treasure is gone. But what you invest in God lasts forever."

These anti-wealth teachings must be tempered with the Christian obligation to provide for the family: But if any provide not for his own, and specially for those of his own house, he hath denied the faith, and is worse than an infidel" (I Timothy 5:8). A man should provide for them while he lives and after he is gone. This is a case for insurance and some savings.

Examples

"In 1956 Jacques Lowe photographed Robert F. Kennedy. Kennedy's father, Joseph, was so impressed with Lowe that he asked him to photograph John F. Kennedy and his wife. Three years later, Lowe became the official photographer of Kennedy's presidential campaign, and after Kennedy was elected, Lowe became his personal photographer.

"Lowe was a very meticulous photographer. He had an estimated 40,000 negatives of images of John F. Kennedy and his family, though only 300-400 photographs were made public. While he was alive, Lowe

Christianity in Crisis
Christ's Plan for Recovery

watchfully monitored the use of his pictures. When a publication or museum wanted prints, he personally took the negatives to the lab for printing. When the job was done, he retrieved them himself.

"Lowe's daughter, Thomasina, said, "He was being more prudent than most. He really believed they were as safe as they could ever be," she said. "He chose to have them there because he was six blocks away from them and he felt psychologically [as if] they were under his bed." "All 40,000 negatives were kept in a safe-deposit vault at the JP Morgan Chase bank branch at 5 World Trade Center, a nine-story building that was heavily damaged in the September 11 attacks. A team of engineers, a 100-ton crane, forklifts, ironworkers, and dump trucks were brought in as part of a plan to move the vault from the second floor. But workers found major fire damage in the vault area; ashes filled the safe-deposit boxes. The only thing that would have survived was metal or stone" ("http://gregburdine.wordpress.com/." "Greg Burdine's Blog").

Christianity in Crisis
Christ's Plan for Recovery

Christianity in Crisis
Christ's Plan for Recovery

Chapter 21

Seek God's Kingdom First

The Command

"But seek ye first the kingdom of God, and his righteousness; and all these things shall be added unto you" (Matthew 6:33).

The Meaning

We must first diligently pursue God's Kingdom and God's righteousness above all earthly needs. This must be done with all diligence. It must be sought with unwavering constancy. It must be sought over home, food, clothing or money.

"By seeking the kingdom of God we are promised all the other things will be added to us. "Of the free bounty, goodness, and liberality of God, without your thought and care, and much less merit; even all these things, meat, drink, clothing, or whatsoever worldly sustenance else is necessary for you: which are not parts of the happiness of saints, only appendages thereunto; which they have over and above what they are, or should be chiefly seeking after" writes John Gill, in his Bible commentary on Matthew 6:33.

God's children are more valuable to Him than the birds, and He takes care of them.

"The ant indeed does, and the bee, and they are set before us as examples of prudence and industry; but the fowls of the air do not; they make no provision for the future themselves, and yet every day, as duly as the day comes, provision is made for them, and their eyes wait on God, that great and good Housekeeper, who provides food for all flesh," declares Matthew Henry. "Take no thought for the morrow, for the time to come. Be not solicitous for the future, how you shall live next year, or

Christianity in Crisis
Christ's Plan for Recovery

when you are old, or what you shall leave behind you. The God that feeds the birds, will surely feed His own children" (http://www.blueletterbible.org/commentaries/comm_view.cfm?AuthorID=4&contentID=1...).

The Example

J Ntiabaao Alita was led to Christ by a worker we supported in Uganda. She visited our meeting of Bible Skills Institute leaders in Jinja and thrilled our hearts with her soft-spoke, earnest testimony. Alita gave me a paper, which said:

"Praise the Lord. I thank the Almighty who has perfected me to be called the child of God. I thank God for the word that I received from Pastor Samuel Moyindo because I received the Word of God and Jesus as my Savior.

"From there, I got a problem with my mother. She chased me from home. I remained homeless because of the Word of Jesus Christ. And yet my father died, so I am in the hands of Pastor Muyinda Samuel (He has taken her into his home and is raising her). "In the year 2005, I didn't study because of school fees." Pray with me." J Ntiabaao Alita.

Pastor Muyinda Samuel provided Alita with a strong Christian home. God provided school funds. Astor Samuel told me Alita is a powerful witness to her teenage friends and is leading many to Christ.

Chapter 22

Judge Not

This is one of the most misused verses in the Bible by those with gross ignorance of the Scripture.

The Command
Jesus commanded, "Judge not, that ye be not judged. For with what judgment ye judge, ye shall be judged: and with what measure ye mete, it shall be measured to you again. (Matthew 7:1, 2).

The Meaning
The word "judge" has two different meanings. It can mean, according to Webster's dictionary, "to pass judgment on." Second, it can be used, again from Webster, "to criticize or censure...to think or suppose, as in "If ye have judged me to be faithful to the Lord" (Acts 26:15). The first, which Christ forbid, means to say, "That drunk ought to go to hell." The second means of judging is to decide what is right and what is wrong. It means to say that man's drunkenness is wrong. This is a righteous judgment encouraged by the Bible. To say that drunkard ought to be put into hell is wrong. Jesus' condemnation of judging was against hypocritical one. There are two other kinds of judging in Scripture that are commanded. A judge has the responsibility of judging. Church discipline is also commanded (Matthew 18:15-20, 1 Corinthians 5:12-13, Galatians 6:1).

Greg Koukl explains, "Appraisals of right or wrong, wise or foolish, accurate or inaccurate, rational or irrational. Such judgment is not forbidden; rather it is commanded. Jesus' instructions "Do not give what

Christianity in Crisis
Christ's Plan for Recovery

is holy to dogs" (Matthew 7:6) require this kind of judgment (What is "holy"? Who are the "dogs"?).

Peter reminds us to "be of sound judgment" since "the end of all things is at hand," (1 Peter 4:7)...We are to judge the deed and not the one who does the deed. Matthew 7:2-5 instructs us not to judge in the sense of condemning the person. It warns us not to try and get a speck of dust out of our neighbor's eye when we have a log in our own eye. The hypocrites were concerned about the sins of other, with no interest in their own sins.

There are a few passages demanding that we judge:

"Do ye not know that the saints shall judge the world? and if the world shall be judged by you, are ye unworthy to judge the smallest matters? Know ye not that we shall judge angels? how much more things that pertain to this life?" (I Corinthians 6:2-3).

Thus saith the LORD; Execute ye judgment and righteousness, and deliver the spoiled out of the hand of the oppressor..." (Jeremiah 22:3).

Judge not according to the appearance, but judge righteous judgment" (John 7:24). Jesus tells us to judge, but to do so righteously. We are to judge 'behavior' by the Bible, not the 'individual.' Judge the deed, not the doer.

Individuals do not have the rights that the government has. Government has rights and responsibilities to judge. Likewise, the church has the responsibility of judging its member.

Christ does not condemn a judge for issuing a sentence, when it is lawful and necessary. "Nor does he condemn our "forming an opinion" of the conduct of others, for it is impossible "not" to form an opinion of conduct that we know to be evil,"...It rather refers to private judgment than "judicial," and perhaps primarily to the customs of the scribes and Pharisees" (says Barnes commentary).

The reason to be careful about judging others, is if we judge others harshly, they will judge us harshly. What is far worse, if we judge harshly, we should expect to be judged by God harshly.

Christianity in Crisis
Christ's Plan for Recovery

Example

A member of the church at Corinth was guilty of fornication and ordered out of the church: "I wrote unto you in an epistle not to company with fornicators: Yet not altogether with the fornicators of this world, or with the covetous, or extortioners, or with idolaters; for then must ye needs go out of the world. But now I have written unto you not to keep company, if any man that is called a brother be a fornicator, or covetous, or an idolater, or a railer, or a drunkard, or an extortioner; with such an one no not to eat. For what have I to do to judge them also that are without? do not ye judge them that are within? But them that are without God judgeth. Therefore put away from among yourselves that wicked person" (I Corinthians 5:9-13).

Christianity in Crisis
Christ's Plan for Recovery

Chapter 23

Clear Your Own Eyes Before You Seek To Help Others

The Command

"Or how wilt thou say to thy brother, Let me pull out the mote out of thine eye; and, behold, a beam is in thine own eye? Thou hypocrite, first cast out the beam out of thine own eye; and then shalt thou see clearly to cast out the mote out of thy brother's eye" (Matthew 7:4, 5).

The Meaning

"If you love your brother it demands that you want to correct some evil in his life," says Providence Baptist Ministries. "If you saw his house on fire you would want him to come out rather than silently let him burn to death. It is just as urgent to call him to abandon some sinful matter that would destroy his soul."

The Pharisees tried to get the splinter out of the eyes of others, when they had a log in their own eye. They appeared to want to help people, but they themselves needed help more than the people they sought to help. They ranted about Jesus healing on the Sabbath while plotting to murder Him!

Before trying to straighten out the life of others, you need to first pray this prayer, "Search me, O God, and know my heart: try me, and know my thoughts: And see if there be any wicked way in me, and lead me in the way everlasting" (Psalms 139: 23, 24).

The Example

The prophet Nathan said to King David, "And there came a traveler unto the rich man, and he spared to take of his own flock and of his own

Christianity in Crisis
Christ's Plan for Recovery

herd, to dress for the wayfaring man that was come unto him; but took the poor man's lamb, and dressed it for the man that was come to him. And David's anger was greatly kindled against the man; and he said to Nathan, As the LORD liveth, the man that hath done this thing shall surely die: And he shall restore the lamb fourfold, because he did this thing, and because he had no pity. And Nathan said to David, Thou art the man. Thus saith the LORD God of Israel, I anointed thee king over Israel, and I delivered thee out of the hand of Saul" (II Samuel 12:4-7).

King David was guilty of taking another man's wife and the prophet Nathan confronted him and sharply said, "Thou art the man." King David became aware of the need to help transgressors by, teaching them God's ways. And he realized he could not help others until he had cleansed his own heart: "Create in me a clean heart, O God. Then will I teach transgressors Thy ways" (Psalms 51:10, 13).

Christianity in Crisis
Christ's Plan for Recovery

Chapter 24

Do Not Offer the Gospel to Reprobates

Few passages are ignored as this one, which commands that we do not continue to offer the gospel to certain people.

The Command

"Give not that which is holy unto the dogs, neither cast ye your pearls before swine, lest they trample them under their feet, and turn again and rend you" (Matthew 7:6).

The Meaning

God commands us to proclaim the gospel to every person. He commands us not to proclaim the gospel again to reprobates who have heard and rejected it over and over.

When our Lord sent out the apostles, He said, "And whoever will not receive you nor hear you, when you depart from there, shake off the dust under your feet as a testimony against them" (Mark 6:11).

Jesus is the 'pearl of great price' that should not be wasted on dogs and swine: "Again, the kingdom of heaven is like a merchant seeking beautiful pearls, who, when he had found one pearl of great price, went and sold all that he had and bought it" (Matthew 13:45-46). There are sinners around us that have sunk to such a nasty state of rejection that God looks upon them as "dogs." and "swine." To tell them again about Christ's salvation is like casting a pearl to a hog; or to give a holy thing to a dog.

In the Bible "dogs" refers to an utterly despicable person (Deuteronomy 23:17-18); a hostile pack against the godly: "The dogs have

Christianity in Crisis
Christ's Plan for Recovery

surrounded Me; the congregation of the wicked has enclosed Me..." (Psalm 22:16; 2 Kings 8:3); those who will be left out of heaven: Revelation speaks of our heavenly home, and says, "But outside are dogs and sorcerers and sexually immoral and murderers and idolaters, and whoever love and practices a lie" (Revelations 22:15).

II Peter 2:22 helps explain this teaching, "But it is happened unto them according to the true proverb, The dog is turned to his own vomit again; and the sow that was washed to her wallowing in the mire." The female hogs get all cleaned up, but returns to wallow in the filthy mire. It represents those who reform morally, but on the inside, they are unconverted. In the end, they reject the Lord and return to their sins.

There are two reasons given for not telling these people about Jesus anymore. One is, it is for their own good. A dog will swallow almost any thing. Pearls could make them ill. By telling a person over and over about God's grace when he doesn't even admit he is a sinner, will only harden him.

Second, a hog can be extremely aggressive. If you gave him a pearl, he might attack you ferociously. Telling serious Muslim about Jesus has cost some Christians their lives.

This does not mean we are not to present the Gospel to every man, at least once. It does mean we are not to continue offering it to those who have thoroughly, reject it. The worst sinners can be saved if they are willing. It means we are not to present the gospel to those who are obstinate; who have rejected it; who are determined not to accept our Lord's grace.

There are those who despise the knowledge of Christ. "The fear of the LORD is the beginning of knowledge: but fools despise wisdom and instruction" (Proverbs 1:7). We should spend our time witnessing to those who appreciate the Gospel, not to those who despise it.

Those God has called and have refused to fear the Lord, reach a point where God will not speak to them: "Then shall they call upon me, but I will not answer; they shall seek me early, but they shall not find me:

Christianity in Crisis
Christ's Plan for Recovery

For that they hated knowledge, and did not choose the fear of the LORD. They would none of my counsel: they despised all my reproof" (Proverbs 1:28-30).

The obedient Christian will humbly and prayerfully discern who is open to the gospel and who is in a reprobate position, not willing to receive Christ or even to listen to His story.

We are urged to ask God for wisdom in this and other matters (James 1:5-8). We must realize that sometimes the right thing to do is to keep our mouth shut. (Philippians 1:8-11). A faithful steward learns when those times are. In the Western World, the church continues to try and attract the unsaved pagans to come to church, to become Christians, though they have rejected the Gospel a hundred times. In the meanwhile, millions who have never heard remain unreached.

Examples

Jesus would not say a single word to the inquiring Herod: "And when Herod saw Jesus, he was exceeding glad: for he was desirous to see him of a long season, because he had heard many things of him; and he hoped to have seen some miracle done by him" Luke 23:8,9). If this had been one of our disobedient modern day disciples, he might have said to Herod, "God loves you and He has a wonderful plan for your life." This man had cut off the head of John the Baptist. Silence was his sentence.

Christianity in Crisis
Christ's Plan for Recovery

Chapter 25

Treat Others
The Way You Want to be Treated

The Command
"Therefore all things whatsoever ye would that men should do to you, do ye even so to them: for this is the law and the prophets" (Matthew 7:12).

The Meaning
The entire law can be condensed into this one sentence. It is a simple way to determine what is right and what is wrong. In knowing how to treat others, put yourself in their situation and decide how you would like to be treated.

This is extremely serious when we see it is commanded in 9 different scriptures, beginning with: "You shall not take vengeance, nor bear any grudge against the children of your people, but you shall love your neighbor as yourself: I am the Lord" (Leviticus 19:18).

Wikidea Encyclopedia says, "The Golden Rule is arguably the most essential basis for the modern concept of human rights, in which each individual has a right to just treatment, and a reciprocal responsibility to ensure justice for others."

A fascinating study on the principle of the Golden Rule was conducted by Bernard Rimland, director of the Institute for Child Behavior Research. Rimland found that "The happiest people are those who help others" (Martin & Diedre Bobgan, How To Counsel From Scripture, Moody Press, 1985, p. 123).

Christianity in Crisis
Christ's Plan for Recovery

We should not do anything to our neighbor we would not want him to do for us. We should always do the things for our neighbor we would like for our neighbor to do for us.

"Christ came to teach us not only what we are to know and to believe, but what we are to do: what we are to do, not only toward God, but toward men; not only toward our fellow disciples, those of our own party and persuasion, but toward men in general, all with whom we have to do" (Matthew Henry).

"It is utterly vain to speak like angels when on our knees before God, if we act like devils in our transactions with men" (Bishop Ryle).

Example

"A certain man went down from Jerusalem to Jericho, and fell among thieves, which stripped him of his raiment, and wounded him, and departed, leaving him half dead. And by chance there came down a certain priest that way: and when he saw him, he passed by on the other side. And likewise a Levite, when he was at the place, came and looked on him, and passed by on the other side. But a certain Samaritan, as he journeyed, came where he was: and when he saw him, he had compassion on him, And went to him, and bound up his wounds, pouring in oil and wine, and set him on his own beast, and brought him to an inn, and took care of him. And on the morrow when he departed, he took out two pence, and gave them to the host, and said unto him, Take care of him; and whatsoever thou spendest more, when I come again, I will repay thee. Which now of these three, thinkest thou, was neighbour unto him that fell among the thieves?" (Luke 10:30-36).

Chapter 26

Ask, Seek, and Knock in Prayer

The Command

"Ask, and it shall be given you; seek, and ye shall find; knock, and it shall be opened unto you: For everyone that asketh receiveth; and he that seeketh findeth; and to him that knocketh it shall be opened" (Matthew 7:7,8).

The Meaning

We should pray, and we should do it as Christ commanded. We are to "ask" as a starving beggar pleads for bread. We are to seek, as a woman seeks the wedding ring she has lost. We must knock as a man knocks on a neighbor's door when his house is on fire.

"Prayer is the appointed means for obtaining what we need, says John Gill the British expositor. "Pray; pray often; make a business of prayer, and be serious and earnest in it. Ask, as a beggar asks alms. Ask, as a traveler asks the way. Seek, as for a thing of value that we have lost; or as the merchantman that seeks goodly pearls. Knock, as he that desires to enter into the house knocks at the door."

We must be relentless in our prayers and make them with desperation, or forget about the entire matter. "Any concern too small to be turned into a prayer is too small to be made into a burden," said Corrie ten Boom (http://www.gather.com/viewArticle.action?articleId=281474978886859).

Christianity in Crisis
Christ's Plan for Recovery

Examples

"Martha Berry was a most persistent young lady who did not know the meaning of "quit." She has a passion to help children of poor landowners and tenant farmers in Georgia get an education. She never married, but devoted her entire life to educating poor children. Her father left her 83 acres of land and she built a small school building. ...

"Seeking money for her project, she approached Henry Ford. He responded by giving her a dime. Other mortals might have been discouraged and accepted failure. But, she took the dime. Bought peanuts. Raised a crop and when she sold it, she paid Mr. Ford back his dime. He was so impressed with her determination that he became a major supporter of her efforts. Ford built the "castle" like dorm at Miss Berry's school, naming it for his wife and mother, Clara and Mary. Later Theodore Roosevelt, Andrew Carnegie, Ellen Louise and Axson Wilson (wife of President Woodrow Wilson) became her supporters.

"Martha Berry died in 1942, leaving behind hundreds of youth she had educated, and the highly-ranked Berry College with excellent education and worthwhile campus work opportunities."

("100 Amazing Answers to Prayer", by William J. Petersen and Randy Petersen (Revell, 2003).

Christianity in Crisis
Christ's Plan for Recovery

Chapter 27

Travel the Narrow Way

The Command

"Enter ye in at the strait gate: for wide is the gate, and broad is the way, that leadeth to destruction, and many there be which go in thereat: Because strait is the gate, and narrow is the way, which leadeth unto life, and few there be that find it" (Matthew 7:13, 14).

The Meaning

"There are but two ways, right and wrong, good and evil; the way to heaven, and the way to hell; in the one of which we are all of us walking: no middle place hereafter, no middle way now: the distinction of the children of men into saints and sinners, godly and ungodly, will swallow up all to eternity" declares the Jamison, Faucett and Brown commentary.

The wrong road to hell is distinguished by being wide and crowded. Wide means it allows those with many lifestyles, moral and religious. Morally, it allows thieves, drunkards, adulterers. Religiously, it allows Buddahist, Muslims, Hindus and all the cults. It is crowded by the great masses of mankind. All but a few are on this road.

By contrast, the right road, the road that leads to heaven is narrow and traveled by few. It is so narrow it is hard to find, "few there be that find it" (Matthew 7:14). As there is a narrow gate that must be entered, and there is a narrow road that must be traveled It is highly crowded, as most people prefer the sinful pleasures it offers.

I learned what it means to walk a narrow path in Africa's Sudan. The North Sudanese Muslims had planted land minds throughout South Sudan. We were instructed not to deviate from the path of the leader who walked on a cleared path. Once in a while we saw a man riding a

Christianity in Crisis
Christ's Plan for Recovery

bicycle, peddling with his hands on a specially rigged bike. He had his legs blow off by a land mind. He was one of the fortunate ones who lived. I was careful not to wander, though there were better looking paths. The way was narrow and sometimes rough, but I stayed on it. The narrow way was the way to live. You could leave it and die.

Romans instructs Christians to mark those who wander from the path of strict doctrine, avoid them as belly worshippers "Now I beseech you, brethren, mark them which cause divisions and offences contrary to the doctrine which ye have learned ; and avoid them. For they that are such serve not our Lord Jesus Christ, but their own belly; and by good words and fair speeches deceive the hearts of the simple" (Romans 16:17-18).

Titus 3:10-11 says heretics get two chances to repent and get back on the path of sound doctrine, or they are to be rejected: "A man that is an heretick after the first and second admonition reject; Knowing that he that is such is subverted, and sinneth, being condemned of himself" (Titus 3:10-11).

Many sinners take comfort in the fact that they are in the midst of the crowd. It should be a source of terrifying alarm, since the crowded way is the way to hell.

Examples

Rudy Atwood "started his career, long ago, playing the piano for Charles E. Fuller and the Old Fashioned Revival Hour. The association was a great one, for Fuller was preaching a solid Bible message, and the music was not contemporary, even by standards of that era. Rudy Atwood bumped into a wall. This was in the form of Charles Fuller's son Dan. This dandy, goodie—two—shoes heretic started Fuller Seminary. Charles Fuller and his wife had been derelict in reigning in the unbelief of their son Dan, and when Dan started Fuller Seminary, Charles Fuller dived right in with his agnostic son.

Christianity in Crisis
Christ's Plan for Recovery

"Rudy Atwood moved along to Youth For Christ. He played for the rallies at the Church of the Open Door in Los Angeles for some years, and then Roy McKewin of Youth For Christ went for the sloppy kiss Christianity which brings in the numbers and saves no one. Rudy Atwood moved on again. He went from ministry to ministry, leaving behind many who would not stay on the narrow way. The last I heard, Rudy Atwood was 94 and teaching piano at Fairhaven College in Michigan, a very narrow Baptist school. ...Today, Rudy Atwood may well be with his Lord in the Glory, but he remains the very icon of Christian piano accompaniment for the narrow way" (Dr. John F. Bailes, Director USA Missions).

Christianity in Crisis
Christ's Plan for Recovery

Chapter 28

Beware of False Prophets

The Command

"Beware of false prophets, which come to you in sheep's clothing, but inwardly they are ravening wolves" (Matthew 7:15)

The Meaning

The Bible foretold that there would be false prophets among us, teaching heresies that would lead people to damnation: "But there were false prophets also among the people, even as there shall be false teachers among you, who privily shall bring in damnable heresies, even denying the Lord that bought them, and bring upon themselves swift destruction" (II Peter 2:1).

"All which agrees very well with the Pharisees, who would have been thought to have been holy and righteous, humble, modest, and self-denying men; when they were inwardly full of hypocrisy and iniquity, of rapine, oppression, and covetousness; and, under a pretense of religion, "devoured widows' houses". These wore a rough garment to deceive' (Zechariah 13:4).

When they were inwardly greedy dogs, grievous wolves, of insatiable covetousness; and, when opportunity offered, spared not the flock to satisfy their rapacious and devouring appetites. The Jews speak of a 'wolfish humility;"

like that of the wolf in the fable, which put on a sheep skin" (Jamerison, Faucett and Brown Commentary).

False prophets pretend to be spokesmen for God. They are corrupt, "whose God is their belly, and whose mind earthly things" (Phillipians 3:18, 19). These prophets are not sent of God. They are denounced by God. False prophets are a sign of the end times, "For there shall arise false Christs, and false prophets, and shall shew great signs and wonders; insomuch that, if it were possible, they shall deceive the very elect" (Matthew 24:24).

Christianity in Crisis
Christ's Plan for Recovery

The Example

Joseph Smith, who founded the Mormon Church, is a perfect example of a false prophet. He and his church teach: '

Mormon doctrine teaches that the god of this universe was once a man just like us. By following the teachings of Mormonism, he was raised from the dead and became a god. He now has his own planet, many wives and children.

They believe that Jesus took three wives while on Earth: Mary, Martha, and Mary Magdalene. They also believe that Jesus fathered many Children during his time on Earth and that Joseph Smith their founder was a direct descendant of Jesus. They believe that after a life of Mormonism and a Mormon marriage has taken place, that when they die they will become gods too. …they will have their own planet, and many goddess wives, and their job for eternity will be to populate the planet. The men want to be a god, they want to rule their own planet. The women want to be eternally pregnant and married to a man, who will be getting other women eternally pregnant (http://www.cbsnews.com/stories/2008/01/31/60minutes/main3775068.shtml).

Christianity in Crisis
Christ's Plan for Recovery

Christianity in Crisis
Christ's Plan for Recovery

Chapter 29

Pray for More Laborers

The Command

"Then saith he unto his disciples, The harvest truly is plenteous, but the labourers are few; Pray ye therefore the Lord of the harvest, that he will send forth labourers into his harvest" (Matthew 9:37-38).

The Meaning

There is a rich harvest of lost souls ready to be harvested for the Lord. The problem is there are not enough laborers to harvest the crop. The crop cannot harvest itself and sinners cannot convert themselves. If they are to be brought into our Lord's kingdom someone must go out and convert the sinners from the error of their ways: " Let him know, that he which converteth the sinner from the error of his way shall save a soul from death, and shall hide a multitude of sins" (James 5:20).

The church complains about the worldly youth, the raging gangs, the rising crimes and the decrease in church attendance, without ever realizing they complain against themselves, about their own lack of prayers for laborers to win them. It is the shame of the church that so many are eager to "perform," to preach, to sing, to act out some play. At the same time, so few are willing to go out and win souls?

The Jamison, Faucett, Brown Bible Commentary suggests two reasons: First, "We miss the compassion of Jesus which gave rise to this request for prayer. Or we simple do not love lost sinners enough to care about their miserable journey into hell.

Second, we believe too little in the power of prayer to bring about definite results." So, in addition to our lack of love for souls there is the lack of faith in our God's promise."

It is a great encouragement to know the harvest is so large and that it is ripe. It is also a great encouragement to know that it is God's work to send the laborers; this is not our responsibility. Our job is to "pray." Isaiah understood this and prayed, "Here am I, send me." (Isaiah. 6:8). It is encouraging to know that the winning of the lost depends on my prayers! God has entrusted you with the right to appeal to Him for laborers and then He sends them.

In Stephen R. Covey's bestselling book on the habits of successful people, he wrote: "Private victories precede public victories. You can't invert that process any more than you can harvest a crop before you plant it." It is through the private victories in the prayer closet that public victories— or harvests of souls, are won.

The Example

In 1806 five college students gathered to pray for mission. The young men were inspired by a dedicated missionary, named William Carey. Their historic prayer meeting would later be labeled the "Haystack Prayer Meeting." These men dedicated themselves to missions and formed the American Board of Commissioners for Foreign Mission. The work struggled until 1895 when thousands of college graduates left home for the mission field. There were as many as ten thousand, some years, that went out to spread the gospel.

Christianity in Crisis
Christ's Plan for Recovery

Chapter 30

Be Wise and Harmless

The Command

"Be ye therefore wise as serpents, and harmless as doves" (Matthew 10:16)

The Meaning

Christ commanded His followers to be wise and harmless. "Behold, I send you forth as sheep in the midst of wolves: be ye therefore wise as serpents, and harmless as doves" (Matthew 10:16).

We are in a hostile territory in which we need all possible wisdom to avoid persecution. We are to do anything to defend ourselves as long as we are harmless as doves.

There is no one in more danger than a sheep in the midst of their greatest enemies—wolves. We are to be wise as serpents, whose cunning is to defend themselves; to defend themselves by hiding.

"Harmless as doves" means to be gentle. The dove simply flies away from trouble. We should be as doves for meekness.

A godly Christian has so much wisdom as to discern his enemy's malice—but so much grace as to conquer his own malice." (http://www.gracegems.org/Watson/wise_as_serpents.htm).

Jesus showed us a demonstration of defensive wisdom in his dealings with His enemy, the Sadducees who were ought to kill Him. They sought to trick Him with a controversial subject—the resurrection, which they did not believe in while the Pharisees did.

"Saying, Master, Moses said, If a man die, having no childen, his brother shall marry his wife, and raise up seed unto his brother. Now there were with us seven brethren: and the first, when he had married a

Christianity in Crisis
Christ's Plan for Recovery

wife, deceased, and, having no issue, left his wife unto his brother: Likewise the second also, and the third, unto the seventh. And last of all the woman died also. Therefore in the resurrection whose wife shall she be of the seven? for they all had her. Jesus answered and said unto them, Ye do err, not knowing the scriptures, nor the power of God. For in the resurrection they neither marry, nor are given in marriage, but are as the angels of God in heaven. But as touching the resurrection of the dead, have ye not read that which was spoken unto you by God, saying, I am the God of Abraham, and the God of Isaac, and the God of Jacob? God is not the God of the dead, but of the living. And when the multitude heard this, they were astonished at his doctrine" (Matthew 22:24-33).

The Example

Thomas Watson wrote, "Moses herein showed a mixture of the serpent and the dove. Miriam murmured against him, Numbers 12:2, 'Has the Lord indeed spoken only by Moses?" Is he the only prophet to declare God's mind to us?" Moses was so wise as to discern her pride and slighting of him—yet so meek as to bury the injury. When God struck her with leprosy, he prayed for her (Numbers 12:13), "Heal her now, O God, I beseech You." And, upon his prayer, she was healed of her leprosy" (http://www.gracegems.org/Watson/wise_as_serpents.htm).

Chapter 31

Take the Yoke With Christ

The Command

"Come unto me, all ye that labour and are heavy laden , and I will give you rest . Take my yoke upon you, and learn of me; for I am meek and lowly in heart: and ye shall find rest unto your souls. For my yoke is easy, and my burden is light." (Matthew 11:28-30).

The Meaning

The word 'yoke' means a bar of wood that unites two animals, enabling them to work in the fields, drawing loads, and pulling farm tools. Before farmers had tractors, yokes were used to link two oxen for plowing. Farmers linked old oxen with young ones to help them and train them. The old ox was able to carry most of the load, until the younger one became stronger.

Figuratively, the yoke is a symbol of practical union. This is made clear by this passage: "Do not be yoked together with unbelievers. For what do righteousness and wickedness have in common? Or what fellowship can light have with darkness? (2 Corinthians 6:14).

Before a person is converted he is linked, or yoked, with sin: "...Do not let yourselves be burdened again by the yoke of slavery" (Galatians 5:1). Jesus commands us to take upon ourselves a yoke that provides "rest," "Take my yoke upon you and learn from me. For I am meek and lowly in my heart and ye shall find rest in your soul" (Matthew 11:28).

We rebel at the idea of a yoke; a yoke is a burden. A yoke means control. A yoke means servitude. But we will bear some yoke, either the wearisome yoke of sin, or the restful yoke of Christ.

Christianity in Crisis
Christ's Plan for Recovery

Christians were saved to serve, to do the work of Christ. Wearing His yoke means doing "His will."

"Take my yoke upon you… ye shall find rest to your souls." "This sound strange--to bid those who are weary from labor to put on a yoke in order to find rest

In the old days, when a farmer wanted to till the ground, he used more than one animal. He would use two horses, two oxen, or two mules so that the work could be done quicker and better. What he usually did was, he would yoke a trained ox with an untrained ox. The trained ox has learned obedience. He will faithfully follow the guidance of the master. The untrained ox still has its determination to do what he wants to do. Its will is not broken, yet. Even with the yoke, it still wants to go its own way. But, the trained ox is stronger and will pull him in the right direction. Gradually it learns the trained ox's obedience. That is the way to fulfill God's eternal purpose in your life--by being yoked with Christ.

The Example

Saul took this yoke upon him when, convicted of his rebellion and conquered by a sense of the Savior's compassion, he said, "Lord, what wouldest thou have me to do?" To take Christ's yoke upon us signifies setting aside of our wills and unconditionally submitting to His sovereignty, acknowledging His Lordship in a practical way. Christ demands something more than lip service from His followers, even a loving obedience to all His commands, "Not every one that saith unto me, Lord, Lord, shall enter into the kingdom of heaven; but he that doeth the will of my Father which is in heaven . . ." (http://www.pbministries.org/books/pink/Gleanings_Godhead/godhead_42.htm).

Chapter 32

Honor Your Parents

The Command

"For God said, 'Honor your father and mother' and 'Anyone who curses his father or mother must be put to death (Matthew 15:4).

The Meaning

This commanded echoes the 10 Commandments, the Old Testament
Exodus 20:12 says, "Honor your father and your mother, so that you may live long in the land the LORD your God is giving you."

Deut. 5:16 commands,"Honor your father and your mother, as the LORD your God has commanded you, so that you may live long and that it may go well with you in the land the LORD your God is giving you."

Again, Ephesians 6:1 tells us, "Children, obey your parents in the Lord for this is just and right. Honour your father and your mother; this is the first commandment with a promise so that all may be well with you and that you may live long on the earth."

Examples

David forgave Absalom for murdering his brother Amnon, and eventually allowed him to return to Jerusalem, Absalom continued to plot and conspire against his father. He gradually turned the people's hearts away from David, towards himself, and drove David from his home and kingdom. II Samuel 18 opens with David's men organizing a war against his father. Despite his humiliation at the hands of his son Absalom, David begs the soldiers, "Deal gently for my sake with the young man Absalom." David showed the best love for the worst of his

Christianity in Crisis
Christ's Plan for Recovery

sons. A son who dishonored his father and lost his life trying to kill his father.

Chapter 33

Settle Disputes

The Command

"Moreover if thy brother shall trespass against thee, go and tell him his fault between thee and him alone: if he shall hear thee, thou hast gained thy brother6But if he will not hear thee, then take with thee one or two more, that in the mouth of two or three witnesses every word may be established. And if he shall neglect to hear them, tell it unto the church: but if he neglect to hear the church, let him be unto thee as an heathen man and a publican" (Matthew 18:5-17).

The Meaning

The flagrant refusal of the modern church to obey this command of Christ is so common few even notice it. Anyone trying to obey this order is looked upon as some radical heretic today. The banner flying over the church is "judge not that you be not judged." The reason Jesus' discipline has disappeared, is the church is sinking into some sort of social club, with very little accountability to God, and even less to the church. This has resulted in few erring members being restored and the church losing its reputation and influence on society. Secular civic clubs have more stringent rules than most churches. They removed members who fail to attend for a year.

"Even when surrounded by stained glass, Christians can stray. A congregation can be less a light to the world, than a mirror of the idolatry, injustice and violence of contemporary North America," noted Ronald J. Allen. This command is to preserve the integrity of the church, recover erring members and resolve conflicts.

Christianity in Crisis
Christ's Plan for Recovery

God tells us exactly what must be done to help an erring brother. This involves a four-step program aimed at restoring the brother and maintaining the reputation of the church.

Step one: "go and tell him his fault between you and him alone." The person who has been harmed by the trespass should take the initiative and go to the offender privately and tell him what he did that offended him. When the offender apologizes you have "gained your brother." You have restored him and strengthened his relationship with the church.

Step two: when the first step fails, "take with you one or two more, that, 'by the mouth of two or three witnesses every word may be established." The hope is he will listen to several people.

Step three ". . . if he refuses to hear them, tell it to the church." When several people establish his guilt, the spiritual family of the church might be able to convince him.

Step four: "...let him be to you like a heathen and a tax collector." The erring member should be put out of the church and dealt with as an unsaved person. Hopefully this will rouse him and get him right.

Purauing Christ instructions restores fallen members, strengthens the church and protects the honor of our Lord. It is essential.

John Leadley Dagg, a prominent 19 Century writer said, "It has been remarked, that when discipline leaves a church, Christ goes with it."

Paul rebuked the Corinthian church for failure to obey Christ in the manner of discipline, "It is reported commonly that there is fornication among you, and such fornication as is not so much as named among the Gentiles, that one should have his father's wife. And ye are puffed up, and have not rather mourned, that he that hath done this deed might be taken away from among you. For I verily, as absent in body, but present in spirit, have judged already, as though I were present, concerning him that hath so done this deed, In the name of our Lord Jesus Christ, when ye are gathered together, and my spirit, with the power of our Lord Jesus Christ, To deliver such an one unto Satan for the destruction of the flesh, that the spirit may be saved in the day of the Lord Jesus. Your glorying is not good. Know ye not that a little leaven leaveneth the whole lump?" (I Corinthians 5:1-6).

It appears that his removal from the early Corinthian church apparently let the immoral man to repentance: "Sufficient in such a man is this punishment, which was inflicted of many" (II Corinthians 2:6).

Examples

I had a pastor friend who enforced this rule within his church. When he heard about two members having a falling out, he would pick up one and take him to the others house. Once inside he would explain we are going to pray and read scripture until your problem is settled. We will not leave the room until this is settled. Bringing the opposing men together and getting them to talk to each other helped resolve disagreements.

A restored brother writes this testimony on the Internet: "I am one of several people I know who have been through church discipline. It was for me a life-saving procedure. Now, many years later, I am grateful for the faithfulness of my church elders and friends who were obedient to Matthew 18 and thus they allowed God to deal directly with me until I came to my senses seven years later. I can assure you that God's discipline can be very severe when necessary. 'It is a fearful thing to fall into the hands of the living God' " (TheParacleteForum.org archive).

Christianity in Crisis
Christ's Plan for Recovery

Chapter 34

Despise Not
The Little Ones

The Command

"Take heed that ye despise not one of these little ones; for I say unto you, That in heaven their angels do always behold the face of my Father which is in heaven" (Matthew 18:10).

The Meaning

They asked Jesus "who is greatest in the kingdom of heaven?" by His disciples. He proceeded to place a little child in their midst of them and taught them the importance of humbling themselves. A child is teachable and willing to depend upon his parents. We must not despise one of these little ones who are privileged to have angels continually watching over them. Also, because the heavenly Father has particular care for the very young.

"For I tell you that their angels in heaven always see the face of my Father in heaven." Angels are the servants of the saints, and they minister to the comfort, and the needs, of the lowest of God's children. They are all ministering spirits, sent forth to minister for those who shall be heirs of salvation.

"In Heaven their angels do always behold the face of My Father." You, little children who read this book, must remember that you are just as much the care of your Good Shepherd now, as were those privileged ones of old who actually saw Him face to face, you must have faith in Him as they had, and believe that though you cannot see Him now, He is still, and always at your side, seeing all you do, hearing all you say,

Christianity in Crisis
Christ's Plan for Recovery

watching over you, and, if you will only let Him, willing to guide you safely to the Home in Heaven which He has gone to prepare for those that love Him and try to do His will" (http://www.apples4theteacher.com/holidays/easter-religious/short-stories/our-savior.html).

John Wesley comments "See that ye despise not one of these little ones - As if they were beneath your notice. Be careful to receive and not to offend, the very weakest believer in Christ: for as inconsiderable as some of these may appear to thee, the very angels of God have a peculiar charge over them: even those of the highest order, who continually appear at the throne of the Most High" **(quoted in: http://christinelouie.theworldrace.org/?filename=dont-despise-these-little-ones).**

The Example

Christine Louie writes from Kenya, "In Africa, I've seen two children named Patrick and Melissa who have been rejected by their parents. Although Patrick is four and Melissa is eight years old, both suffer from disabilities and are only the physical size of a two year old. Both can hardly talk and only make sounds while Melissa cannot walk because she is too weak. When Philip and Aidah (two of our amazing hosts) had taken them in, they told us how they had to deworm them, help them use the restroom, and try to help them eat. They have improved much through love, care, and prayer. These are the implications of extreme neglect of children, but love is turning things around" (http://christinelouie.theworldrace.org/?filename=dont-despise-these-little-ones).

Christianity in Crisis
Christ's Plan for Recovery

Chapter 35

Never Stop Forgiving

The Command

"Then came Peter to him, and said, Lord, how oft shall my brother sin against me, and I forgive him? till seven times? Jesus saith unto him, I say not unto thee, Until seven times: but, Until seventy times seven" Matthew 18:21, 22).

The Meaning

"The Jewish rule required people to forgive three times, but not a fourth. So Peter asked if seven times would be adequate, which seemed very generous to him. Jesus showed the extent of forgiveness is, by telling Peter, 'I do not say to you, up to seven times, but up to seventy times seven' (Matthew 22). "He means that we are not to limit our forgiveness to a specific number of times. As often as someone offends us and asks forgiveness, we should extend it. Further, even if he does not ask forgiveness, we should forgive him and treat him properly, setting the right example" (Jamerison, Faucet and Brown Commentary).

Jesus instructs us that we should not have a limit on forgiveness. Even if a man does not ask to be forgiven, we should still forgive him. Though our fallen nature screams for revenge, we must not seek it. Throughout history men have parroted Jesus teaching on forgiveness:

"Forgiveness is the scent that the rose leaves on the heel that crushes it" said Arnott.

Forgiveness ought to be like a canceled note--torn in two and burned up so that it never can be shown against one," wrote Paul Boese.

"Little vicious minds abound with anger and revenge and are incapable of feeling the pleasure of forgiving their enemies." – Lord

Christianity in Crisis
Christ's Plan for Recovery

Chesterfield "If one by one we counted people out For the least sin, it wouldn't take us long To get so we had no one left to live with. For to be social is to be forgiving" said George Herbert.

"To carry a grudge is like being stung to death by one bee" (William H. Walton).

"I will forgive, but I won't forget" is just another way of saying, "I will not forgive."

Example

"On Monday morning, October 2, 2006, a gunman entered a one-room Amish school in Nickel Mines, Pennsylvania. In front of twenty-five horrified pupils, thirty-two-year-old Charles Roberts ordered the boys and the teacher to leave. After tying the legs of the ten remaining girls, Roberts prepared to shoot them execution with an automatic rifle and four hundred rounds of ammunition that he brought for the task. The oldest hostage, a thirteen-year-old, begged Roberts to 'shoot me first and let the little ones go.' (http://astore.amazon.com/spiritualitya-20/detail/0787997617)

"Refusing her offer, he opened fire on all of them, killing five and leaving the others critically wounded. He then shot himself as police stormed the building. His motivation? 'I'm angry at God for taking my little daughter,' he told the children before the massacre" (Amish Grace: How Forgiveness Transcended Tragedy (amazon), by Donald B Kraybill, Steven M Nolt and David L Weaver-Zercher).

When the Amish offered forgiveness to the killer's family, attended his funeral and started a support fund for the killer's wife and three children it captivated the media. The story of "Amish forgiveness" appeared in 2,900 newspaper stories, on 534,000 web sites and drew dozens of TV crews to the little Amish village.

Chapter 36

Do Not Divorce

The Command

"And said, For this cause shall a man leave father and mother, and shall cleave to his wife: and they twain shall be one flesh? Wherefore they are no more twain, but one flesh. What therefore God hath joined together, let not man put asunder" (Matthew 19:5, 6).

The Meaning

"For the LORD, the God of Israel, saith that he hateth putting away" (Malachi 2:16).

The Pharisees objected to this on the basis that Moses had allowed divorce.: "When a man hath taken a wife, and married her, and it come to pass that she find no favour in his eyes, because he hath found some uncleanness in her: then let him write her a bill of divorcement, and give it in her hand, and send her out of his house" (Deuteronomy 24:1).

Jesus said, "He saith unto them, Moses because of the hardness of your hearts suffered you to put away your wives: but from the beginning it was not so" (Matthew 19:8). "Moses tolerated divorce when a woman's life was endangered," writes Matthew Henry.
God's command to honor marriage is widely ignored in the United States: Dating websites for cheaters appear on the Internet, urging, "Life is short. Have an affair." Eighty percent of those who divorced remarry within three years and 65 percent of those marriages will end in divorce. "Over a million children each year are involved in divorce and more than 13 million children under 18 live with one parent. These single-parent families are growing at a rate twenty times faster than two-parent

Christianity in Crisis
Christ's Plan for Recovery

families" (http://answers.yahoo.com/question/index?qid=20061117092914AAtlpR).

    Jesus demanded that we honor marriage by not putting away our mate and marrying another, except for fornication, or sexual unfaithfulness (Matthew 5:32).

    Paul seem to add another obvious exception, "abandonment." "If the unbelieving depart, let him depart. A brother or a sister is not under bondage in such cases: but God hath called us to peace" (I Corinthians 7:10-15). It one party leaves the other they have ended the marriage and left the other party free from any bondage to the marriage.

    If you suspect this is the writing of a divorced man, let me assure you my wife, Betty, and I have been married for over 63 years at the time of this writing.

Example

    Golfer Tiger Woods and Governor Arnold Schwarzenegger, head a list of famous men admitting they have committed adultery. As a result they lost their families, their reputation and a fortune in money. "After leaving the governor's office I told my wife about this event, which occurred over a decade ago," Schwarzenegger said Monday night in a statement to The New York Times. "I understand and deserve the feelings of anger and disappointment among my friends and family. There are no excuses and I take full responsibility for the hurt I have caused. I have apologized to Maria, my children and my family. I am truly sorry" (http://www.breitbart.com/article.php?id=D9N9AAD00&show_article=1).

Chapter 37

Always Tell the Truth

The Command

Jesus said, "Thou shalt not bear false witness" (Matthew 19:18).

The Meaning

The Bible says in Romans 13:13, "Let us walk honestly, as in the day; not in rioting and drunkenness, not in chambering and wantonness, not in strife and envying." The dictionary defines this "honesty" as: "honorable in principles, intentions, and actions; upright and fair."

Dishonesty comes directly from the Devil: John 8:44 says: "Ye are of your father the devil, and the lusts of your father ye will do. He was a murderer from the beginning, and abode not in the truth, because there is no truth in him. When he speaketh a lie, he speaketh of his own, for he is a liar, and the father of it" (John 8:44).

Watch your words. Be careful what you say, lest you misspeak and lie. Satan is the father of lies. "Little white lies," are big, abominable lies that take you to the lake of fire" (Amazing Grace Web site).

The average person lies several times a day; with insincere compliments like, "that dress looks great on you"; lies to yourself like, "that was not my fault;" lies to your parents like, "I did real well on that test;" lies to your mate like "I did not have anything to drink."

Honesty makes you feel terrific about yourself and creates trust in others. It improves your relationship with yourself and others. Most important, it shows Christ you love Him.

Christianity in Crisis
Christ's Plan for Recovery

Examples

The greatest and most deadly lie ever told, is the great lie told by Muslims. It is called "Al-taqiyya," which means to lie when it is an advantage to the cause of Islam. The Muslim's Holy Book is the only one that endorses lying. Qur'an 24:11 says, "Of a truth, they who advanced that lie were a large number of you; but regard it not as an evil to you. No, it is an advantage to you."

In countries where they are not in control, they declare "Islam is a religion of peace." They prove this is a lie whenever they gain control of a country.

Muhammad made a truce with the Jewish Koraish tribe. The truce was all a lie. In 628 C.E., Muhammad slaughtered the entire unarmed, defenseless tribe of hundreds.

Christianity in Crisis
Christ's Plan for Recovery

Chapter 38

Guard Against False teaching

The Command

"Mark 8:15 KJV

And he charged them, saying , Take heed , beware of the leaven of the Pharisees, and of the leaven of Herod." (Mark 8:15).

The Meaning

This teaching was somewhat confusing to the disciples because they had never heard of 'leaven' referring to doctrine, or teaching.

Mark, instead "of the leaven of the Sadducees", says, "the leaven of Herod"; either because Christ might caution against all three; or because the Sadducees were generally Herodians, taking Herod to be the Messiah; or were on his party, or for his government, which the Pharisees disliked; and the Herodians were generally Sadducees. By "the leaven" of these is meant their doctrine, as appears from (Matthew 16:12).

The doctrines the Pharisees taught were the commandments and inventions of men, the traditions of the elders, free will, and justification by the works of the law: the doctrine of the Sadducees was, that there was no resurrection of the dead, nor angels, nor spirits: now because they sought secretly and artfully to infuse their notions into the minds of men; and which, when imbibed, spread their infection, and made men sour, morose, rigid, and ill natured, and swelled and puffed them up with pride and vanity, Christ compares them to leaven; and advises his disciples to look about them, to watch, and be on their guard, lest they should be infected with them (John Gill's Exposition of the Bible).

Christianity in Crisis
Christ's Plan for Recovery

The Examples

Our world is drowning in false teachings.
- The 'health and wealth teaching' declaring prosperity in the name of the 'homeless,' poor Jesus.
- The Catholic teaching that they have power on earth to forgive sins.
- The popular Calvinist teaching that Jesus did not die for everyone.
- The Mormon teaching that a man can become a God.
- The Armenian teaching that a man can save himself by his own good works.

Chapter 39

Pray With Faith

"Now in the morning as he returned into the city, he hungered. And when he saw a fig tree in the way, he came to it, and found nothing thereon, but leaves only, and said unto it, Let no fruit grow on thee henceforward for ever. And presently the fig tree withered away. And when the disciples saw it, they marvelled, saying, How soon is the fig tree withered away!" (Matthew 21:18-20).

The disciples marveled at Jesus power when He caused a fig tree to wither.

The Command

"Jesus answered and said unto them, Verily I say unto you, If ye have faith, and doubt not, ye shall not only do this which is done to the fig tree, but also if ye shall say unto this mountain, Be thou removed, and be thou cast into the sea; it shall be done. And all things, whatsoever ye shall ask in prayer, believing, ye shall receive" (Matthew 21:21-22).

The Meaning

Jesus amazed the disciples by causing a fig tree to wither. He amazed them further by telling them, they could see miraculous answers to their prayers, if they had faith.

"But this is a proverbial expression; intimating that we are to believe that nothing is impossible with God, and therefore that what he has promised shall certainly be performed" (http://biblecommenter.com/matthew/21-22.htm).

Christianity in Crisis
Christ's Plan for Recovery

Faith can only operate where there is a promise of God. It can only operate in the realm of God's will. I cannot pray with faith for God to move a mountain, because God has not promised to move a mountain. If He promised to move it, I could pray in faith and it would move. I can pray for the Lord to forgive my sins because He has promised to forgive them.

To obtain things in prayer, two things are required. One, you must have a promise from God that He will do it. Two, you must believe that promise. Even Jesus could not pray in faith to escape His crucifixion. He had to say, "Father, if thou be willing, remove this cup from me: nevertheless not my will, but thine, be done" (Luke 22:42).

To pray without knowing the will of God makes impossible to have faith. To pray without faith, when we know God's will, is to doubt God. One prayer we can pray, knowing it is God's will, for sinners to be delivered from evil: "Who gave himself for our sins, that he might deliver us from this present evil world, according to the will of God and our Father" (Galatians 1:4).

The Examples
Brenda Hoeve was once an atheist who became a believer. She had a grandmother, an aunt, and a school teacher who prayed for her. She lost her job when her prefabrication housing company went bankrupt. A coworker asked her to help with a job for the Methodist pastor.

She liked this pastor and decided to take her children to the church. After the service, the pastor gave her a New Testament. She was converted the next morning, while reading the Gospel of Matthew.

Brenda declared, "Since that day in June of 1972, when I first met Jesus, I have prayed for my loved ones. Prayer brought me into His Kingdom, and I pray it will bring others in the Kingdom."

(Read the complete testimony at: http://www.precious-testimonies.com/BornAgain/h-k/HoeveBrenda.htm).

Chapter 40

Render to Caesar And God What is Their's

The Command

"Then saith he unto them, Render therefore unto Caesar the things which are Caesar's; and unto God the things that are God's" (Matthew 22:19-21).

The Meaning

The Jews sought to trap Jesus with a tax question, which answered 'yes' or "no' would have put Him in big trouble. Jesus avoided the trap by asking for a coin. When they produced one, Jesus took it and asked, "Whose image and inscription is this?" By calling the crowd's attention to a graven image on the coin, He discredited the tax issue.

"The coin bearing Caesar's image was explained by the famous saying: "Render to Caesar the things that are Caesar's, and to God the things that are God's."

"In the Hebrew tradition, everything rightfully belonged to God. By using the words, "image and inscription," Jesus has already reminded His interrogators that God was owed exclusive allegiance and total love and worship" (http://www.lewrockwell.com/orig11/barr-j1.1.1.html).

As Dorothy Day is reputed to have said, "If we rendered unto God all the things that belong to God, there would be nothing left for Caesar."

However, true Christians have to be upstanding citizens, "Submit yourselves to every ordinance of man for the Lord's sake: whether it be to the king, as supreme Or unto governors, as unto them that are sent by him for the punishment of evildoers, and for the praise of them that do well. For so is the will of God, that with well doing ye may put to silence

Christianity in Crisis
Christ's Plan for Recovery

the ignorance of foolish men: As free, and not using your liberty for a cloke of maliciousness, but as the servants of God. Honour all men. Love the brotherhood. Fear God. Honour the king" (I Peter 2:13-17).

Again, Scripture says, "For this cause pay ye tribute also: for they are God's ministers, attending continually upon this very thing. Render therefore to all their dues: tribute to whom tribute is due; custom to whom custom; fear to whom fear; honour to whom honour" (Romans 13:6–7).

The Example

The first personal income tax was imposed in Egypt. Pharaoh, the ruler of Egypt had a dream that foretold seven years of plenty followed by seven years of famine (Genesis 41). Joseph instructed the king to tax the agricultural profit for twenty-percent and save it up. When the seven years of famine came, there was food for the people.

Joseph, a servant of God, set up the first recorded personal taxation. It was in a pagan land with an ungodly ruler. When the famine came, the Egyptians had food and were even able to assist the neighboring countries. The taxation was an institution of God raise up to save the people from starvation.

Chapter 41

Be a Servant to Others

The Command

"But whosoever will be great among you, let him be your minister (Matthew 20:26).

The Meaning

"Then came to him the mother of Zebedee's children with her sons, worshipping him, and desiring a certain thing of him. And he said unto her, What wilt thou? She saith unto him, Grant that these my two sons may sit, the one on thy right hand, and the other on the left, in thy kingdom. But Jesus answered and said, Ye know not what ye ask. Are ye able to drink of the cup that I shall drink of, and to be baptized with the baptism that I am baptized with? They say unto him, We are able. And he saith unto them, Ye shall drink indeed of my cup, and be baptized with the baptism that I am baptized with: but to sit on my right hand, and on my left, is not mine to give, but it shall be given to them for whom it is prepared of my Father." (Matthew 20:20-23).

Jesus explained, "Ye know that the princes of the Gentiles exercise dominion over them, and they that are great exercise authority upon them. But it shall not be so among you: but whosoever will be great among you, let him be your minister; And whosoever will be chief among you, let him be your servant: Even as the Son of man came not to be ministered unto, but to minister, and to give his life a ransom for many" (Matthew 20:25-28).

Christianity in Crisis
Christ's Plan for Recovery

To be a servant of someone means to yield yourself to them to obey them Know ye not, that to whom ye yield yourselves servants to obey, his servants ye are to whom ye obey: whether of sin unto death, or of obedience unto righteousness? (Romans 6:16). To be a servant of God would mean you have submitted yourself to God's authority and that you obey His commands.

John Wesley wrote, ""Do all the good you can, by all the means you can, in all the ways you can, in all the places you can, at all the times you can, to all the people you can, as long as you ever can."

George Muller said, "A servant of God has but one Master. It ill becomes the servant to seek to be rich, and great, and honored in that world where his Lord was poor, and mean, and despised."

"The Church has earned the reputation of being concerned only for itself. Others have concluded this because the answer to every question is to do something else for ourselves; let's pray more, let's conduct another city-wide prayer and worship event, let's build another building, let's tell people what we think about this issue, and so on. It is always about us. If we are going to become an agent of spiritual and social transformation it is going to have to be about them!" (Jack Dennison, NPPN Newsletter, April 2002).

The Example

This story illustrates being a good servant, "A rich man sent his servant to the marketplace, and there the servant came upon a beggar. The beggar fell to his knees and cried out, "Please sir, might you spare some of your master's money so that I might have a bite to eat?" The servant replied, "What have you done for my master that you should be given some of my master's money? Is there no good that you can do in the world that you must grovel at my feet and beg?

"The servant walked away giving the beggar nothing, for the servant had nothing of his own to give. The beggar followed the servant to the rich man's home. He began working in the master's fields for free. He

Christianity in Crisis
Christ's Plan for Recovery

weeded the fields. He planted the seeds. He watered and pruned the vines. He gathered the grapes at harvest time, and pressed the grapes into wine.

"When the rich man heard about what the beggar was doing, he sent his servant to bring the beggar to him. "What shall I do with the beggar?", the servant asked. The rich man replied, "He is no longer a beggar, but is my son. Bring him into my home, he shall eat with me!" ("The Beggar's Lesson", unknown source; this version comes from Lynn Tracci).

Christianity in Crisis
Christ's Plan for Recovery

Chapter 42

Love the Lord

The Command

"Master, which is the great commandment in the law? Jesus said unto him, Thou shalt love the Lord thy God with all thy heart, and with all thy soul, and with all thy mind. This is the first and great commandment" (Matthew 22:36-38).

The Meaning

This is the first and greatest of commandments because obedience to all the rest must flow from our love of God. An extraordinary love for Him is above all things.

We are to love God for three reasons: First, Because He is the Greatest of the Greats, "Who is like thee, glorious in holiness, fearful in praises, doing wonders? (Exodus 15:11).

Second, because of all His benefits to us. Psalms 103 lists 10 of these benefits: "Bless the LORD, O my soul, and forget not all his benefits: Who forgiveth all thine iniquities; who healeth all thy diseases; Who redeemeth thy life from destruction; who crowneth thee with lovingkindness and tender mercies; Who satisfieth thy mouth with good things; so that thy youth is renewed like the eagle's. The LORD executeth righteousness and judgment for all that are oppressed. ...the LORD is merciful and gracious, slow to anger, and plenteous in mercy...He hath not dealt with us after our sins; nor rewarded us according to our iniquities" (Psalms 103:1-10).

Third, because He loves us enough to give the life of His son to die for us. "We love him, because he first loved us" (I John 4:19).

Christianity in Crisis
Christ's Plan for Recovery

The Example

Tricia Goyer writes, "When did you fall in love with God? That's my question for the day. And to explain my answer I need to tell you a lit bit about my story. I grew up going to church for the most part. It started when I was eight-years-old, and my mother and grandmother gave their hearts to the Lord. They attended a church where people attended together yet they also reached out to each other outside of the church building. I remember picnics and dinners out. I remember a new community of people who surrounded our family with love. I remember my Sunday School teacher who shared God's love through flannel graph stories and films. Not the VCR tapes movies, but rather the old reel-to-reel films that showed the parables of Jesus, and told what it meant to be faithful, honest, and true. I loved my Sunday School class, children's church, and the prizes I got for memorizing Scripture. I remember singing songs about God. I remember sensational Summer VBS camps and memorizing the books of the Bible to win a board game.

"The problem was that while all those things made me think about God (and I loved Him in a way), I didn't understand what a personal relationship God meant. I didn't know how it applied to my everyday life.

"And then, instead of continuing my relationship with God, and continuing to spend time with others, I walked away from that in my teen years. I wanted to do things my own way. I was looking for love and I thought I could find it in boys. Instead, I found myself pregnant and without a boyfriend when I was only 17. For many, many months I didn't want to think about what God thought about me. I tried to push all thoughts of Him out of my mind. I didn't want to think about all the memory verses I'd memorized as a child. Instead, I wallowed in everything I had lost--my youth, my teen years, my boyfriend who was with someone else. I felt more and more depressed as they days passed.

"Then one day about noon I was watching soap operas and I started to remember those good moments when a church family loved me. I

Christianity in Crisis
Christ's Plan for Recovery

didn't dwell on everything that had gone wrong. This day, I thought about a time in my life when things used to be right, when I was happy. When I believed in God, and when I had joy. And that is the day I gave my heart to the Lord...my whole heart. I wrapped my arms around my stomach and I said, "God, I have messed up big time. If you can do anything with my life, please do." It was at that moment that I felt HOPE spring into my heart. Hope in God. Hope in my future. Hope in eternity because I knew Christ had forgiven me for all my sins. And that was the beginning of my love relationship with God. I had loved him before like I loved peanut butter and jelly sandwiches and loved watching CHIPS on TV. Not potato chips, but those cute highway patrolmen who rode around on motorcycles and stopped crime.

"Once I realized the depth of my sin, and understood had God had washed me and made me are pure and white as snow, that's when I truly fell in love with him. By accepting my sin and the pain it caused, I truly fell in love with Jesus for taking that sin away through His death on the cross." (a blog by author Tricia Goyer, http://triciagoyer.blogspot.com/2011/05/when-did-you-fall-in-love-with-god.html).

Christianity in Crisis
Christ's Plan for Recovery

Chapter 43

Love Your Neighbor

The Command
"You shall love your neighbor as yourself" (Matthew 22:39).

The Meaning
Jesus had this discussion with a man, "Master, which is the great commandment in the law? Jesus said unto him, Thou shalt love the Lord thy God with all thy heart, and with all thy soul, and with all thy mind. This is the first and great commandment. And the second is like unto it, Thou shalt love thy neighbour as thyself. On these two commandments hang all the law and the prophets" (Matthew 22:36-40).

This command is given throughout the Bible, stressing its importance: "Thou shalt not avenge, nor bear any grudge against the children of thy people, but thou shalt love thy neighbour as thyself: I am the Lord" (Leviticus 19:18).

Jesus commanded us to love our neighbor as ourselves. This is one of the most repeated commands given to us. Eight times the Bible repeats it:

Thou shalt not avenge, nor bear any grudge against the children of thy people, but thou shalt love thy neighbour as thyself: I am the LORD" (Leviticus 19:18).

Honour thy father and thy mother: and, Thou shalt love thy neighbour as thyself" (Matthew 19: 19).

"If there is any other commandment, are all summed up in this saying, namely, "You shall love your neighbor as yourself" (Romans 13:9).

For all the law is fulfilled in one word, even in this: "You shall love your neighbor as yourself" (Galatians 5:14).

Christianity in Crisis
Christ's Plan for Recovery

"If you really fulfill the royal law according to the Scripture, "You shall love your neighbor as yourself," you do well" (James 2:8).

Christians love must be in deed and not just in word: "My children, our love should not be just words and talk; it must be true love, which shows itself in action" (1 John 3:18).

This command strips bare the hypocrisy of those who merely say they love God. "If a man say, I love God, and hateth his brother, he is a liar: for he that loveth not his brother whom he hath seen, how can he love God whom he hath not seen? (I John 4:20).

Jesus said men must love their neighbor as their self. Men naturally set their affections on themselves — on corrupt, self-loving, self-centered self. While some use this passages to promote loving yourself, Jesus taught that to be His disciple, you must deny yourself, crucify yourself and bury yourself by your baptism. Knowing that men naturally love themselves above all else, he set this self-love as the measure of how much they should love their neighbor.

The Example

One Good Samaritan has saved 144 people from suicide in China. "One bridge over China's Yangtze River sees hundreds of suicides as the country's rate rises — though fewer since a Nanjing man started spending weekends there saving lives" writes Matt Dents of 'Newser.' "With 280,000 killing themselves ever year — twice the US total — Chen Si has so far stopped 144 suicides, the Los Angeles Times reports. "All people really need is one person willing to lend a hand," Chen says. The Chinese Samaritan says, "I always have to tell them there is nothing I can't solve," Chen says, though "it's a lie" he tells them this to keep them from despair. Sadly, there were 50 he failed to save.. (http://www.newser.com/tag/29012/1/good-samaritan.html).

Chapter 44

Be Ready for Christ's Return

The Command

"Therefore be ye also ready: for in such an hour as ye think not the Son of man cometh" (Matthew 24:44).

The Meaning

With only a brief time to live, our Lord chose to urge His hearers to be "ready" for His return. Being ready means to be prepared to enter heaven by a conversion, a work of God's grace in the heart. In addition, it means to be prepared to receive abundant rewards for faithful service.

Matthew Henry pointed out the urgency of being ready for Christ's return, "Nothing is more sure than that Christ will come a second time, to judge both quick and dead; and happy will those be that are ready; they will be received by Christ into everlasting habitations, and be forever with him: and miserable will those be, who will not be ready..."

It is most important to all the disciples of Christ to be awake, to stay awake and to mind their own duties.

This command came in the last sermon Jesus ever preached. It was the subject He chose, exhorting men to be ready for His return and to stay out of hell, as He approached His death.

At Christ's return, or at our death, we will either enter an eternal heaven, or an eternal hell. There will be no second chance.

The Example

"I haven't spoken to my mother in 5 years." These words spoken through quivering lips by a woman in Bristol, Virginia. Following a sermon on the return of Jesus Christ the lady made her way to the

Christianity in Crisis
Christ's Plan for Recovery

church altar, fell on her knees, and cried to God to save her. Afterwards, she told me, "I have asked God to forgive me. Now, I am going straight to the phone and ask my mother to forgive me. I cannot face the Lord without getting my heart right."

Christianity in Crisis
Christ's Plan for Recovery

Chapter 45

Watch for Christ's Return

The Command
"Therefore keep watch, because you do not know on what day your Lord will come" (Matthew 24:42).

The Meaning
To watch for Christ's coming, is to maintain a constant attitude of expectancy. It means when He comes you will not be surprised. Watching for Christ's return means you stay aware of the Bible signs leading to the Lord's return.

There are two basic reasons for watching for Christ's return. One is because His coming will be sudden, without any warning. The other is, no one knows the day or hour when He will come.

Over and over Christ told us to watch for His return. All our attention should be focused on this. The Bible is filled with reminders:

"Watch therefore, for ye know neither the day nor the hour wherein the Son of man cometh" (Matthew 25:13).

"Take ye heed, watch and pray, for ye know not when the time is" (Mark 13:33).

"Watch ye therefore: . . . Lest coming suddenly, He find you sleeping" (Mark 13:36).

"Unto them that look for Him shall He appear the second time without sin unto salvation" (Hebrews 9:28).

"Abide in Him; that, when He shall appear, we may have confidence, and not be ashamed before Him at His coming" (I John 2:28).

"And what I say unto you I say unto all, Watch" (Mark 13:37).

Christianity in Crisis
Christ's Plan for Recovery

The Example

William Rice, pastor of Calvary Baptist Church in Clearwater, Florida explained his view on proper burial, "My opinion is that to bury our dead in the ground, according to historic Christian tradition does provide a powerful testimony, a witness, of the hope that is ours in Christ. My own preference is that when I die, that I may be buried (in a pine box or burlap sack I do not care) facing the eastern sky as one last act of faith, as one final act of proclamation, that I believe in the power of the one who rose from the dead and who will one day keep His promise to raise me, and all who belong to Him, when He returns to redeem His own and establish His eternal kingdom"

(http://www.calvarybaptist.org/pages/page.asp?page_id=73903&articleId=12174).

Chapter 46

Observe the Lord's Supper

The Command

And as they were eating, Jesus took bread, and blessed it, and brake it, and gave it to the disciples, and said, Take, eat; this is my body. And he took the cup, and gave thanks, and gave it to them, saying, Drink ye all of it" (Matthew 26:26-27).

The Meaning

Jesus served supper to His disciples, the night before his crucifixion. And He ordered His disciples to repeat this in remembrance of Him. The Lord's Supper is to remember Christ's past work for us on the cross and to remember His second coming. He brake it, and said, Take, eat: this is my body, which is broken for you: this do in remembrance of Me. After the same manner also He took the cup, when He had supped, saying, This cup is the new testament in My blood: this do ye, as oft as ye drink it, in remembrance of Me. For as often as ye eat this bread, and drink this cup, ye do show the Lord's death till He come."

It was on the night the Jews celebrated their miraculous deliverance from slavery in the land of Egypt. Christ is to the Christian a far greater Passover feast, celebrating our deliverance from the slavery of sin: "For even Christ, our Passover, is sacrificed for us: Therefore let us keep the feast, not with old leaven, neither with the leaven of malice and wickedness; but with the unleavened bread of sincerity and truth" (1 Corinthians 5:7, 8).

Christ broke the bread, which was the symbol of His body which would be broken for our sins. The body of Christ is represented by bread; he said, "I am the bread of life" (John 6:35).

Christianity in Crisis
Christ's Plan for Recovery

The breaking of the bread symbolizes the breaking of Christ's body. We are commanded to do this in remembrance of His body being broken on Calvary: 'That the Lord Jesus the same night in which he was betrayed took bread: And when he had given thanks, he brake it, and said, Take, eat: this is my body, which is broken for you: this do in remembrance of me" (I Corinthians 11:23, 24).

Christ explained that the reason for this is to "remember" His body being broken for their deliverance. We symbolize receiving Christ into our bodies as we eat. Just as bread gives physical life, Christ gives us spiritual life as we take Him into our lives by faith. Christ served the disciples wine, saying, "For this is my blood of the New Testament. The Old Testament was confirmed by the blood of bulls and goats (Heb. 9:19, 20; Ex. 24:8). "For when Moses had spoken every precept to all the people according to the law, he took the blood of calves and of goats, with water, and scarlet wool, and hyssop, and sprinkled both the book, and all the people, Saying, This is the blood of the testament which God hath enjoined unto you" (Hebrews 9:19-20). The blood on the doorpost in Egypt, on the night of the Passover, only saved "the children of Israel" (Leviticus 16:34), but Christ is a propitiation for the sins of the whole world" (1 John. 2:2).

The Lord's Supper is a treasured time when Christians gather to remember the great sacrifice their Lord made and the great salvation it brought them. Just as the bread symbolized the body of Christ, the wine symbolized the blood of Jesus Christ. He shed His blood for us once for all. Christ declared, "It is finished!" Nothing more can be added to His bloody death. We take the wine to remember His atoning blood. "In whom we have redemption through his blood, the forgiveness of sins, according to the riches of his grace" (Ephesians 1:7).

The Example

Luxian took his final Lord's Supper in prison. He was held in stocks with his legs far apart. His captors arranged for him to remember his

Christianity in Crisis
Christ's Plan for Recovery

Lord's last supper. It would last be his last supper. To Luxian and others about to be martyred, taking the Lord's Supper was extremely important.

In a Charthage prison, on March 6, A.D. 203, two Christians converted their last meal into a holy Lord's Supper. The next day they were executed because they refused to renounce their faith. (From 'The Soul of the Symbols,' Eerdmans Publishing Co., 1966, pages 172-174).

Christianity in Crisis
Christ's Plan for Recovery

Chapter 47

Baptize My Disciples

The Command

"Go ye therefore, and teach all nations, baptizing them in the name of the Father, and of the Son, and of the Holy Ghost" (Matthew 28:19).

The Meaning

Peter obeyed Christ's command and baptized the converts on the day of Pentecost: "Then Peter said unto them, Repent, and be baptized every one of you in the name of Jesus Christ for the remission of sins, and ye shall receive the gift of the Holy Ghost. For the promise is unto you, and to your children, and to all that are afar off, even as many as the Lord our God shall call . And with many other words did he testify and exhort, saying, Save yourselves from this untoward generation. Then they that gladly received his word were baptized: and the same day there were added unto them about three thousand souls " (Acts 2:38-41).

Philip obeyed this command when he won an Ethiopian eunuch to Christ. "And the eunuch answered Philip, and said, I pray thee, of whom speaketh the prophet this? of himself, or of some other man? Then Philip opened his mouth, and began at the same scripture, and preached unto him Jesus. And as they went on their way, they came unto a certain water: and the eunuch said, See, here is water; what doth hinder me to be baptized? And Philip said, If thou believest with all thine heart, thou mayest. And he answered and said, I believe that Jesus Christ is the Son of God. And he commanded the chariot to stand still: and they went down both into the water, both Philip and the eunuch; and he baptized him" (Acts 8:34-38).

The Example

It was a baptism service that scared me. Back in the 1950s I was in an evangelistic crusade, in Old Harbor Bay, Jamaica. It coincided with their annual "Believer's Day.' I marveled at the testimonies they gave at the church and when they were finished they started marching up to the top of the hill singing, "We Are Marching to Zion." When we arrived at the peak, there was a small pool where they were preparing to baptize. The people were so excited they were pushing and crowding to get a good view of the baptisms. Then, this was what was scary. They climbed into trees hardly strong enough to support them. I had trouble focusing on the water because I was afraid a limb would break at any minute. None did. But I left amazing at the excitement the Jamaicans had over people following Christ in baptism. It impressed on me that every baptism should be just as exciting.

Chapter 48

Proclaim the Gospel

The Command

"And he said unto them, Go ye into all the world, and preach the gospel to every creature" (Mark 16:15).

The Meaning

"And he said unto them, Go ye into all the world, and preach the gospel to every creature. He that believeth and is baptized shall be saved; but he that believeth not shall be damned" (Mark 16:15-16).

God holds Christians responsible for spreading the Gospel and winning people to Christ. "Brethren, if any of you do err from the truth, and one convert him; let him know that he which converteth the sinner from the error of his way shall save a soul from death, and shall hide a multitude of sins" (James 5:19-20).

"And they that be wise, shall shine as the brightness of the firmament; and they that turn many to righteousness as stars for ever and ever." (Daniel 12: 3).

"For though ye have ten thousand instructors yet have ye not many fathers: for in Christ Jesus I have begotten you through the Gospel" (I Corinthians 4:15).

Christian must face their responsibility for the salvation of mankind throughout the world.

The Apostle Paul declared, "Yet when I preach the gospel, I cannot boast, for I am compelled to preach. Woe to me if I do not preach the gospel! If I preach voluntarily, I have a reward; if not voluntarily, I am simply discharging the trust committed to me" (I Corinthians 9:16, 17).

Christianity in Crisis
Christ's Plan for Recovery

The Example

Bitakatahire Blazio, the Bible Skills Institute Director in the Congo and Western Uganda reported on a most unusual conversion. He writes that, "John and students of BSI preached to a Muslim witch doctor. The response was not what they hoped for. He terrified them by putting a curse on them and said they would be dead in seven days. Like Elijah battling the prophets of Baal, the witch doctor prayed to Allah for their deaths and they prayed in Jesus name for his conversion. In seven days, the students were still alive. However, the witch doctor's son died on the third day. He called the students to come. When they did, he gave his life to Christ." These men have tremendous influence in Africa. a well known witch doctor is converted, it influences many others to follow his example.

Chapter 49

Make Disciples Among all Nations

The Command

"And he said unto them, Go ye into all the world, and preach the gospel to every creature" (Mark 16:15).

The Meaning

Missions were not a mere part of the early church's ministry, but the ministry itself. "After the fall of Jerusalem (70) through the year 180, almost all the important Mediterranean areas, such as Rome in Italy, Antioch in Syria, Carthage in North Africa, and Alexandria in Egypt, had been evangelized. By 200, North European countries such as France and England had been (in part) Christianized," writes Kim, Young Do.

"This section of Scripture is known as the Great Commission," writes Mary Fairchild. "As the last recorded personal directive of the Savior to his disciples It is the foundation for evangelism and cross-cultural missions work."...the Lord has commanded us to put our faith in action."

The famed missionary David Livingstone, answered those who resisted the Great Commission because of the "sacrifice" required, "If a commission by an earthly king is considered a honor, how can a commission by a Heavenly King be considered a sacrifice?"

"No one has the right to hear the gospel twice, while there remains someone who has not heard it once," cried Oswald J. Smith.

"The command has been to 'go,' but we have stayed -- in body, gifts, prayer and influence. He has asked us to be witnesses unto the uttermost parts of the earth...but 99% of Christians have kept puttering around in the homeland." (Robert Savage, Latin American Mission).

Christianity in Crisis
Christ's Plan for Recovery

Here is William Booth's response to those who say they have not been called: "'Not called!' Did you say? 'Not heard the call,' I think you should say. Put your ear down to the Bible, and hear Him bid you go and pull sinners out of the fire of sin. Put your ear down to the burdened, agonized heart of humanity, and listen to its pitiful wail for help. Go stand by the gates of hell, and hear the damned entreat you to go to their father's house and bid their brothers and sisters and servants and masters not to come there. Then look Christ in the face -- whose mercy you have professed to obey--and tell Him whether you will join heart and soul and body and circumstances in the march to publish His mercy to the world." (William Booth, founder of the Salvation Army).

Either we must go, or we must support those who do go.

The Example

Jim Elliot had a burden to reach the Auca Indians in Equador. These were a fierce people who were killers. They threw spears that took the lives of Elliot and the missionaries with him. They had guns, but decided it was better to die and leave the Aucas with another chance to know Christ. Before going to the mission field, Jim said, "He is no fool who gives what he cannot keep, to gain what he cannot lose." Later his wife and others went back and won most of the tribe to Christ.

Christianity in Crisis
Christ's Plan for Recovery

Chapter 50

Practice Self-Denial

The Command
"And he said to them all, If any man will come after me, let him deny himself, and take up his cross daily, and follow me"(Luke 9:23).

The Meaning
The first step in following Jesus Christ is to deny yourself. The love of self is the essence of evil. This is the root of sin. It is the essence of ungodliness. The denial of self is the essence of godliness. This is the root of righteousness. It is the essence of godliness.

If you want to follow Jesus, it means putting your feet in the foot prints of Christ. They lead to self-denial, to a cross and to the loss of all things.

"You can longer go to the places you want, read the material you want, watch the TV shows you want, or spend your money the way you want—you must deny self."
Robert Schuller, founder of the Glass Cathedral, said, "It is precisely at this point that classical theology has erred in its insistence that theology be God-centered and not man-centered" (From Schuller's book "Self Esteem the New Revolution, quoted at:

http://www.rapidnet.com/~jbeard/bdm/exposes/schuller/quotes-se.htm).

This wide spread, popular teaching is the blatant contradiction of the teaching of Jesus Christ. Schuler said build up yourself. Jesus said deny yourself.

Self-denial is a truth that upsets money-centered preachers. They prosper by preaching health, wealth, peace, self-esteem and happiness. Talk of self-denial is not mentioned.

"We must live a life of self-denial, mortification, and contempt of the world; we must not indulge our ease and appetite, for then it will be

Christianity in Crisis
Christ's Plan for Recovery

hard to bear toil, and weariness, and want, for Christ...we must prefer the salvation and happiness of our souls before any secular concern whatsoever," writes Matthew Henry.

Jesus made the necessity of self-denial unmistakable when He said, "So likewise, whosoever he be of you that forsaketh not all that he hath, he cannot be my disciple" (Luke 14:32-34).

This is a bitter truth to those who love things other than Christ: "This know also, that in the last days perilous times shall come. For men shall be lovers of their own selves, covetous...lovers of pleasures more than lovers of God" (II Timothy 3:1-4).

Jesus set the example of self-denial. He was a homeless man. He had to catch a fish to pay his taxes, borrow a coin to illustrate a sermon. He even refused the drugging drink on the cross that could have eased His pain. Let's get real. Ignore the modern Christians about you. True Christianity means denial of yourself. The first rule of Christianity is you cannot be a Christian and do what you want to do. You cannot go to places you wants to. You cannot look at the things you want to. You cannot spend your money the way you want.

The Example

"Hazel Miner, a schoolgirl, and her two little brothers attended a small school in rural North Dakota in the early part of this century. One day in March, 1919, a blizzard roared in after the children were already at school and the drifts began piling up. Class was dismissed early and the three children started for home in their buggy.

"Along the way, the buggy turned over and they could not right it. After the horse got loose, they took shelter from the wind and blowing snow under the overturned buggy. Hazel wrapped the two little boys in blankets, and they waited for help. Soon it got dark and they realized that probably no one would be able to find them until the next day.

"During the night Hazel took off her coat and spread it over her sleeping brothers and then lay down on top of them to keep them warm. When they were rescued the following afternoon, the two little fellows were fine. Their sister was still lying on top of them. They didn't know she had frozen to death.

"That's what Jesus did--He died that we might live" (PrayerNet Newsletter, Jul 18, 1997).

Christianity in Crisis
Christ's Plan for Recovery

Christianity in Crisis
Christ's Plan for Recovery

Chapter 51

Keep Yourself From Covetousness

Jesus was addressing two brothers fighting over an inheritance. He warns them about coveting the things of this world.

The Command
"And he said unto them, Take heed, and beware of covetousness" (Luke 12:15).

The Meaning
Thomas Aquinas said of covetousness: "it is a sin directly against one's neighbor, since one man cannot over-abound in external riches, without another man lacking them...it is a sin against God, just as all mortal sins, inasmuch as man contemns things eternal for the sake of temporal things."
(http://atheism.about.com/od/christianhistory/ig/Seven-Deadly-Sins-Punishments).

Jesus is the "Pearl of Great Price." But greed seeks to place material things first in our hearts.

Caesar Kalinowski explains, "Hey my neighbor left his wife and married a beautiful woman half his age. I am a good looking guy, I should be able to do the same...my friend ditched her old, run of the mill, average husband and found herself a rich man who gives her everything. I think I deserve to be spoiled too!" "Oh the marriages that have ended because the grass appeared greener on the other side! It may not even be the seemingly perfect spouse of someone else that is coveted. It might be the freewheeling, do what you want lifestyle of a single

Christianity in Crisis
Christ's Plan for Recovery

person who has no family responsibilities and comes and goes as they please that is coveted" (http://www.christian-divorce-support-online.com/causes-of-divorce.html).

Covetous leads to divorce and theft, adultery and even murder. This was the case with King David. "And it came to pass in an eveningtide , that David arose from off his bed, and walked upon the roof of the king's house: and from the roof he saw a woman washing herself; and the woman was very beautiful to look upon. And David sent and enquired after the woman. And one said, Is not this Bathsheba, the daughter of Eliam, the wife of Uriah the Hittite? And David sent messengers, and took her; and she came in unto him...and the woman conceived, and sent and told David, and said, I am with child...David wrote a letter to Joab, and sent it by the hand of Uriah. And he wrote in the letter, saying , Set ye Uriah in the forefront of the hottest battle, and retire ye from him, that he may be smitten , and die...and Uriah the Hittite died" (II Samuel 11:2, 3, 4, 5, 14-16).

This all came from desiring what belongs to someone else. This is forbidden in the 10 Commandments (Exodus 20:17). To a covetous person, it is unthinkable for someone to have a nicer wife, home, car, clothes or vacation than he has. It drives him to get more than he needs or can ever use.

The Example

There is a story about a peasant who complained to a giant landowner about how unfair it was that the landowner owned every bit of the land. The landowner promised to give the peasant all the land he could walk around in a whole day, knowing the nature of men. The peasant, greedily trying to take in all the area possible, overexerted himself and dropped dead with a heart attack. He ended up with nothing, a victim of covetousness.

Chapter 52

Feed the Poor

The Command

"Then said he also to him that bade him, When thou makest a dinner or a supper, call not thy friends, nor thy brethren, neither thy kinsmen, nor thy rich neighbours; lest they also bid thee again, and a recompence be made thee. But when thou makest a feast, call the poor, the maimed, the lame, the blind: And thou shalt be blessed; for they cannot recompense thee: for thou shalt be recompensed at the resurrection of the just" (Luke 14:12-14).

The Meaning

When we have a dinner we should invite the poor, those who are in need. If we just invite the wealthy, it may profit us socially. Inviting the poor can give us joy. Nehemiah said, "Go and enjoy choice food and sweet drinks, and send some to those who have nothing prepared. This day is sacred to our Lord. Do not grieve, for the joy of the LORD is your strength" (Nehemiah 8:10).

Feeding the rich can feed our pride and make us feel important. Ahasuerus put on a pompous display, "At that time King Xerxes reigned from his royal throne in the citadel of Susa, and in the third year of his reign he gave a banquet for all his nobles and officials. The military leaders of Persia and Media, the princes, and the nobles of the provinces

Christianity in Crisis
Christ's Plan for Recovery

were present. For a full 180 days he displayed the vast wealth of his kingdom and the splendor and glory of his majesty" (Esther 1:2-4).

You should not feel like a looser by feeding people who cannot afford to return the invitation. Heaven is preparing a feast for Jesus' followers beyond anything the mind of man can conceive.

The Example

My greatest Christmas memory is of my Grandmother Dean. She was a hard worker; gardening, raising chickens and cooking. At Christmas, she worked frantically preparing dinner for her extended family. Before she served the meal, she would get me to help her carry some of the food to several poor families. She saw that poor families got a nice Christmas meal before she fed her own family.

Christianity in Crisis
Christ's Plan for Recovery

Chapter 53

Exercise Humility

The Command

"But when thou art bidden, go and sit down in the lowest room" (Luke 14:10).

The Meaning

Jesus taught a parable on humbling yourself by taking the lower position at a wedding feast: "And he put forth a parable to those which were bidden, when he marked how they chose out the chief rooms; saying unto them, When thou art bidden of any man to a wedding, sit not down in the highest room; lest a more honourable man than thou be bidden of him; And he that bade thee and him come and say to thee, Give this man place; and thou begin with shame to take the lowest room. But when thou art bidden, go and sit down in the lowest room; that when he that bade thee cometh, he may say unto thee, Friend, go up higher: then shalt thou have worship in the presence of them that sit at meat with thee. For whosoever exalteth himself shall be abased ; and he that humbleth himself shall be exalted" (Luke 14:7-11).

Prominent men were always seated to take the top seats at Biblical feasts. If someone of lesser prominence took a top seat, and a more prominent man came in, he was asked to move. Our Lord commanded that a man should humble himself and take a lower seat. He would not be embarrassed, by being told to get up and move to a lower seat. The wise Solomon, gave the same advice, "Stand not in the place of great men, for better it is that it be said unto thee, Come up hither, than that thou shouldest be put lower" (Proverbs 25:6, 7), We must humble ourselves rather than exalt ourselves.

Christianity in Crisis
Christ's Plan for Recovery

"A person may behave humbly towards God yet be proud. `Ahab put on sackcloth and fasted and went softly' (I Kings 21:27), but his heart was not humble. A man may bow his head like a bullrush, yet lift up the ensigns of pride in his heart" ([From The Godly Man's Picture by Thomas Watson, a Puritan Paperback edition published by the Banner of Truth.)

"A humble soul thinks better of others than of himself: 'let each esteem other better than themselves' (Phillipians 2:3). A humble man values others at a higher rate than himself and the reason is because he can see his own heart better than he can other's. He sees his own corruption and thinks surely it is not so with others; their graces are not so weak as his; their corruptions are not so strong. `Surely', he thinks, `they have better hearts than I.' A humble Christian studies his own infirmities and another's excellences and that makes him put a higher value upon others than himself. `Surely I am more brutish than any man' (Proverbs 30:2). Paul, though he was the chief of the apostles, still calls himself 'less than the least of all saints' (Ephesians 3:8).

Example

"A person may behave humbly towards others, yet be proud. Who was more humble than Absalom in his outward behaviour? `When any man came near to do him obeisance, Absalom took him by the hand and kissed him'" (II Samuel 15:5). Though he acted humbly, he aspired to take away his father's crown: `As soon as ye hear the sound of the trumpet, then ye shall say, Absalom reigneth in Hebron' (II Samuel 15:10). Here, was pride dressed in humility's mantle. His pride led him to his death.

Christianity in Crisis
Christ's Plan for Recovery

Chapter 54

Make the Church A House of Prayer

The Command

"Saying unto them, It is written, My house is the house of prayer: but ye have made it a den of thieves" (Luke 19:46).

The Meaning

The place where Christians assemble is to be called a "house of prayer." This command is found in the Old Testament, as well as the New,: "Even them will I bring to my holy mountain, and make them joyful in my house of prayer: their burnt offerings and their sacrifices shall be accepted upon mine altar; for mine house shall be called an house of prayer for all people" (Isaiah 56:7).

When Christians gathered to worship outdoors, by a river, they considered it 'a place where prayer was to be made': "And on the sabbath we went out of the city by a river side, where prayer was wont to be made; and we sat down, and spake unto the women which resorted thither" (Acts 13:13).

We are commanded to call a place for Christians to gather, a "house of prayer."

The command is accompanied by this rebuke "Their house of prayer had become a "den of thieves:" "Is this house, which is called by my name, become a den of robbers in your eyes? Behold, even I have seen it, saith the LORD" (Jeremiah 7:11).

The temple money changers exchanged currency from many different countries so the worshippers could purchase animals to offer as sacrifices in the temple. The money changers were not honest in their

Christianity in Crisis
Christ's Plan for Recovery

exchanges of currency—they were stealing by paying them less than their money was worth. "The priests lived, and lived plentifully, upon the altar; but, not content with that, they found other ways and means to squeeze money out of the people; and therefore Christ here calls them thieves, for they exacted that which did not belong to them," wrote Matthew Henry.

These religious thieves were not only stealing money from the people; they were also robbing God of His glory.

Today, very little time is spent praying in churches. They have turned church auditoriums into entertainment centers, where talented guests "perform," and the people applaud. One wealthy athlete was asked why he charged churches $10,000 to give his "testimony." He replied, "If those Christians are dumb enough to pay it, I am dumb enough to take it." The bigger the name of the entertainer, the bigger the crowds. And the bigger the crowds, the bigger the offerings.

Jesus plainly told us, "Freely ye have received, freely give." Christ gave us our salvation freely, and we should give our testimonies and music "freely." Try and find a Christian who is a drawing card that will come "freely." They charge. The churches usually hide the amount of the fees from the congregation. If the members knew how much their "guests" were being paid it would not only destroy their credibility, but also create trouble in the church.

Religious places are being turned into dens of thieves. As the prophet Jeremiah said, "Is this house, which is called by my name, become a den of robbers in your eyes? Behold, even I have seen it, saith the LORD" (Jeremiah 7:11).

The Example

The Vatican in Rome is a house impressing the poor masses with their great wealth. Prayer may have help build it, but selling "indulgences" sure helped finance it. Indulgences were a main spark that fueled the reform. Martin Luther was right when he said that there was abuse of indulgences. The compendium to the Catechism says:...unfortunately the practice of indulgences has on occasion been improperly applied. This has been either through "untimely" and superfluous indulgences which humiliated the power of the keys and weakened penitential satisfaction or it has been through the collection of "unlawful profits" which blasphemously took away the good name of indulgences...(Indulgentiarum Doctrina, 8).

"'Indulgences are nothing more than a permission to sin. It is a money-making exercise through which Catholics think they can buy their way into heaven!' An indulgence is simply a remission through the infinite merits of Jesus Christ and His Saints of the temporal punishment due for sins committed after guilt and eternal punishment have been remitted." (www.ourcatholicfaith.org).

The money changers at Jerusalem's temple could have wished to have prospered as well as the Catholics.

Christianity in Crisis
Christ's Plan for Recovery

Chapter 55

Receive the New Birth

The Command

Jesus said, "Ye must be born again" (John 3:7).

The Meaning

Jesus gave this command during a conversation with a devout Jewish leader named Nicodemus: "Now there was a man of the Pharisees named Nicodemus, a member of the Jewish ruling council. He came to Jesus at night and said, 'Rabbi, we know you are a teacher who has come from God. For no one could perform the miraculous signs you are doing if God were not with him.' In reply Jesus declared, 'I tell you the truth, no one can see the kingdom of God unless he is born again.' 'How can a man be born when he is old?' Nicodemus asked. 'Surely he cannot enter a second time into his mother's womb to be born!' Jesus answered, 'I tell you the truth, no one can enter the kingdom of God unless he is born of water and the Spirit. Flesh gives birth to flesh, but the Spirit gives birth to spirit. You should not be surprised at my saying, "You must be born again." The wind blows wherever it pleases. You hear its sound, but you cannot tell where it comes from or where it is going. So it is with everyone born of the Spirit'" (John 3:1-8).

Though this command is given to one man, Nicodemus, Jesus applied it to all men. All men are born depraved, shaped in iniquity. A second birth is required to give them a new nature. Christ said a man cannot "see" the kingdom of heaven--he cannot understand it without being born again by the Spirit of God. This is the malady, the great sickness of the human race. All men are born with an evil nature. Though it is a surprised to parents, governments and churches, it still

Christianity in Crisis
Christ's Plan for Recovery

breaks forth in horrific acts. Only when Christ enters the human heart by His Spirit can this be changed.

Christ bluntly added no one can ever enter heaven without this transforming birth: Even the most moral, most religious person will never get to heaven unless he experienced this new birth.

The Example

Jake De Shazer was a pilot in the famous Dootlittle Raid that bombed Japan near the end of WWII. He crashed in China and was taken prisoner. They tortured him and starved him in the Shanghai prison camp.

After the war, Jake returned to Japan was a missionary. He was handing out tracts titled "I Was a War Prisoner of Japan" outside Tokyo's Shibuya Station. Mitsuo Fuchida, the only Pearl Harbor pilot to live through the war, took received a tract. Fuchida, who led the attack on Pearl Harbour, read the tract, was "born again," and became an outstanding evangelist.

Jake De Shazer turned a bitter enemy into a Christian brother and coworker. (Read full story in Pulpit Helps, Oct 1991. Pages 2-3).

Chapter 56

Feed My Sheep

The Command

Jesus commanded, "Feed my sheep" (John 21:16).

The Meaning

"So when they had dined, Jesus saith to Simon Peter, Simon, son of Jonas, lovest thou me more than these? He saith unto him, Yea, Lord; thou knowest that I love thee. He saith unto him, Feed my lambs. He saith to him again the second time, Simon, son of Jonas, lovest thou me? He saith unto him, Yea, Lord; thou knowest that I love thee. He saith unto him, Feed my sheep" (John 21:15-16).

Three times Jesus asked Peter if he loved him (Jesus). Three times Peter said yes, and three times Jesus responded with, "Feed my sheep" (John 21:15-17). Many Christians believe that attending church and praising God is all that they need to do. The Apostle Peter praised Jesus and proclaimed his love for Christ. (Matthew 26:33). Jesus responded by telling Peter that if he loved Him, he should 'feed His sheep.'

Miles Wesner said, "When a baby is hungry, you can yell at him or spank him, and he may quit crying momentarily, but you haven't filled his need. In fact, you've increased his need. He's still hungry, but now he's also frightened and hurt and confused! The baby needs a balanced diet of good food and so does the Christian. A forty year old man lying in a crib nursing a bottle is a tragedy. A forty year old Christian sitting in a church pew demanding traditional platitudes is a worse tragedy!" (http://www.diversitypress.com/s081405.html).

It is the duty of a minister to feed his sheep a steady, healthy diet of God's Word.

Christianity in Crisis
Christ's Plan for Recovery

The Example

An old farmer at a church convention laughed when he read the program. "Preacher," he said, "It's funny how you folks go at this church business. You've had sermons and talks all day long on how to get people to attend church. "Now, I've never heard a single speech at a farmers' convention on how to get cows to come up to the trough. Instead, we devote all our time learning what to put in the trough. We try to decide on the best kind of feed! I sorta have a notion that if you put in more time discussin' what to put in the trough, you wouldn't have to spend all that time on how to get folks to come to church!" (http://www.diversitypress.com/s081405.html).

Christianity in Crisis
Christ's Plan for Recovery

CPSIA information can be obtained
at www.ICGtesting.com
Printed in the USA
FFOW02n2250160115
10262FF

9 780972 591553